WARTS AND ALL

Polly wanted a room-warming party, but the first objection would be money. Her mother might fairly say that if she was giving it she should pay. She hadn't noticed any Saturday jobs going recently – perhaps she could charm a few warts.

The more she thought about the idea the better it seemed. If she advertised her services in the personal column of the local paper it could all be managed by post. She could use a box number and remain completely anonymous. She spent some time drafting advertisements in her head and finally got it down to ten words: *Wart charming by post. Sixpence a wart. Send postal order.*

3 cde

Also by Rodie Sudbery

RICH AND FAMOUS AND BAD

and published by CAROUSEL BOOKS

Rodie Sudbery

Warts And All

Carousel Editor: Anne Wood

CAROUSEL BOOKS
A DIVISION OF TRANSWORLD PUBLISHERS LTD
A NATIONAL GENERAL COMPANY

WARTS AND ALL

A CAROUSEL BOOK 0 552 52039 X

Originally published in Great Britain
by André Deutsch Limited

PRINTING HISTORY
André Deutsch edition published 1972
Carousel edition published 1973

This book is set in Intertype Baskerville

Carousel Books are published by Transworld Publishers Ltd.,
Cavendish House, 57–59 Uxbridge Road,
Ealing, London, W.5.

Made and printed in Great Britain by
Cox & Wyman Ltd, London, Reading and Fakenham

NOTE: The Australian price appearing on the back cover is the recommended retail price.

To Cluty

Warts and All

I

Polly was woken by a terrible noise. She huddled into the pillow unable to think what it might be, or indeed do anything but wish for it to stop.

'Switch it off. Switch it off!' said the voice of Jennifer, sleepy and cross.

Remembering, Polly leaned out of bed and groped for the clock which lay on the floor under a pudding basin. Covering it had been the only way to pacify Jennifer's outrage the evening before when she discovered she was expected to share a room with something that ticked so loudly.

'I shall need an alarm clock when I'm at the tech,' Polly had told her mother.

'The journey won't take much longer, will it?'

'That's not the point. I don't want to go off in a rush every morning and arrive late half the time. Being called was all very well for school, but I'm going to be responsible for waking myself from now on.'

'Good,' was all her mother had said; and later she had produced a dusty spare clock from the top of her wardrobe.

Jennifer seemed to have gone straight back to sleep. Polly stretched out between the warm sheets and yawned; then coiled up her resolution and bounced out of bed.

Her hair, washed the evening before, looked distressingly wild in the bathroom mirror. She parted it with wet fingers and was glad when the reflection became obscured by steam. Her father tried the door as she was drying herself, rattling it in disbelief. He was unused to getting the bathroom anything but first.

'Shan't be a minute,' she called.

He never spoke much in the morning, but she presumed he had heard. Her clothes lay waiting where she had left them ready in her room: brown jersey, mustard skirt, new tights, and new shoes of a pale indeterminate shade intended to go with everything. Dressing took longer than usual because she treated everything with care.

After ten minutes' brushing in front of the broken mirror propped on top of the chest of drawers one side of her hair still refused to lie flat. Dashing to the bathroom when her father came out she ran the hot tap over her brush and tried again.

'Why are you doing that?' asked Jennifer.

'Go and wash.' The back of her jersey was a bristling mat of loose hairs. She took it off and removed them one by one.

'Is your hair wet?' asked her mother at breakfast.

'No,' said Polly, studying her timetable as she ate to check that she had put the right books in her new case. Luckily her satchel had been so dilapidated that the question of whether or not she could use it at the tech hadn't arisen.

'Won't you be rather warm in what you've got on?'

'Warm?' Polly gazed in consternation at the sunshine outside. She had planned her clothes weeks before; an autumn ensemble for the autumn term. 'I don't think so.'

'You'll boil,' said her young brother Hugh. 'You're pink already.'

She ran a finger round the inside of her polo neck without replying.

'What's for breakfast?' asked Jennifer, coming in. 'Mummy, Jonathan's crying like anything.'

'I know. I can't possibly deal with him until I've got the rest of you off.'

Polly went upstairs, entering her parents' room in passing and giving the baby a bottle of pills from the dressing table to play with. Her hair, now dry, had regained its awkward kink; wrapping her night-dress round her shoulders she attacked it again with the brush.

'Shouldn't you be leaving, Polly?' called her mother.

Her arm ached and she seemed to have prickly heat. She tore off her jersey and found a pale grey blouse. Then her skirt was wrong and she had to put on a black pinafore dress. Although it wasn't what she'd planned she quite liked this set; she fancied it made her look rather like a demure French schoolgirl. Sparing a giggle for the oddness of wanting to look like any kind of schoolgirl she ran downstairs.

'Where's my case?'

'Where you left it,' returned her mother automatically. 'Is that it under Michael's blazer? Have you got your purse? You shouldn't really have spent so long eating if you were going to change your clothes. Jennifer, how many times have I told you not to feed Hairy from the table. Run along then, love. You look very nice. Have a good day.'

'Bye,' said Polly.

Stilwell's technical college was at the top of a hill. Polly toiled upwards, changing her case from hand to hand with ever-increasing frequency. Large numbers of people were going the same way as her, but none were going so fast. She overtook several conversations.

'. . . I found out about that girl, Rex, but I'm afraid she's engaged.'

'Not to worry; harder work, that's all.'

'I do like your way of putting things!'

Polly didn't.

'He's packed me up. He said to me "You're too babyish, you take things too seriously, and you're two-timing it." Well I know I take things seriously and I am a bit babyish, but I wasn't two-timing it.'

She did look rather babyish. Her front teeth were too large for her mouth, as though they had only just come through.

'The Doctor really cares whether you pass or not.'

'He does.'

An earnest pair of boys; Polly went through the swing doors just ahead of them. The electric clock in the entrance hall said one minute to nine. She stood for a moment pretending to adjust her watch. Everyone seemed to know where they were going except her. There were more boys than girls but the girls were more alarming; they all looked about twenty, whereas the hard-faced boys in their leather jackets and jeans might only have been eighteen. Polly noticed with relief a little window with a porter behind it.

'Room 43?' he said. 'Round to the right on the ground floor. There's a plan of the building over there on the wall, look. That'll show you everything you want to know.'

The clock hand jumped to nine. Polly decided the plan could wait and hurried off to the right.

Everyone glanced up for a moment as she entered the classroom. She made for the nearest empty place and sat down. There was enough talking going on for her to be quietly inconspicuous while taking stock. The girls looked much the same as the ones outside, but the boys were reassuringly ordinary and young, even if one did have a lock of grey hair in front.

'What's your name, Dad?' he was asked.

'Alsop.'

'I'm Sandy and this is Boris.'

Sandy was small and cheeky. His own hair was red. Polly's neighbour had a coil of a rich and improbable brown. Her face was glamorous and her laugh loud. Polly was glad that her attention remained turned the other way until the lecturer came in.

'Good morning,' he said. 'I'm Dr. Makepiece. As you may know I'm in charge of the full time ordinary level course. First of all I'd like to welcome you all to the technical college, and by the way you're not expected to stand up when I come into the room. You don't stand up when you speak to me either. You do call me sir, or Dr. Makepiece, whichever you prefer.' He wrote Makepiece on the board in block capitals.

'The next thing is book lists. Have you all got book lists?'

Polly was surprised they hadn't all got books. She had assembled everything on her list some weeks ago and most of it was in her case at this moment; the timetable wasn't very specific about what might be required.

There were several other things. Smoking was one.

'The rule of the ordinary level course is no smoking. I realize that you are all at least fifteen, but you can console yourselves with the thought of the benefit to your lungs. If you've ever seen a photograph of the lungs of a smoker in cross section...'

Working hard was another. He himself would be taking them for algebra, he said. There wasn't much time for algebra that morning.

'Hell's bells!' said Polly's neighbour at the end of the hour.

'He really cares whether you pass or not,' said Polly. 'That's what I heard someone say,' she added quickly, but she was speaking to a turned head.

A double line on Polly's timetable divided the lectures at this point, which as Dr. Makepiece had just explained signified a break. Polly went with the stream as they left the room and presently found herself in the canteen on the end of a queue. The tables were rapidly filling and the noise was considerable. They were drinking tea; Polly found the idea unusual but not unwelcome.

She was standing behind a group of girls which included her erstwhile neighbour, whose name seemed to be Liz. Liz talked more than the others and louder.

'How old are you?' she called.

'Fifteen,' said Polly, when it appeared this was meant for her.

'You were right after all, Hilary. Hilary said you must be or you couldn't be here. You look much younger, don't you?'

'Do I?'

The queue shifted and brought Liz to the counter, where she delved in her handbag for coppers and paid with them one by one. Polly opened her case, leaning it awkwardly against one leg, and extracted her purse in readiness.

'How many sugars, dear?' she was asked.

'One please.'

The boy behind her asked for four.

'Cost you extra.'

'You'll be lucky.'

Polly slid her purse into her pocket, picked up her case in one hand, and balanced cup and saucer in the other while she looked round for somewhere to sit. She saw Sandy and Boris in a corner and then her eye was caught by another face, familiar but unexpected: surely it was Kim – she couldn't remember his surname – Kim the friend of her friend Judith's brother, and of her old school enemy Louise. She had supposed him still to be at the grammar school with Mark. He was glancing at her in recognition; yes, it was Kim, debonair as ever. Last time they met had been in a crowded café.

Remembering how he had given her his chair on that occasion she looked away in sudden embarrassment lest he should think she expected him to do the same now. She didn't feel like following the example of Liz, who was perched on the edge of a table swinging her long legs, apparently unperturbed by the virtual disappearance of her skirt. There was a noticeboard on the wall; she went to stand by it. Gulping hot tea she read: DANCE TO JIM BICKS AND THE FRENETIC FOUR IN THE HALL EVERY MONDAY LUNCHTIME 1–2 P.M. There was also *Rollerskate for Oxfam!* and 'Wanted, guitarist. Apply J. Bicks.' Then they would be the frenetic five, she supposed.

She took her empty cup back to the counter because she couldn't think what else to do with it, and received surprised thanks. Leaving the canteen she found her way to the main entrance and had a good look at the plan. It showed the whereabouts of a cloakroom; she thought she might spend the rest of the break peacefully combing her hair.

She found it full of girls draped over the basins, chatting as they smoked. She bolted herself into a lavatory, needing privacy like air. There was a swollen cigarette stub disintegrating horribly in the pan.

'... I said to Peter, my lashes are very thick, and he said "Oh are they, I've never noticed." Just like a man!'

Polly pushed between two girls to wash her hands, thus gaining a portion of mirror. Propping her case on the basin amid silence she scrabbled under her books for a comb and pulled it quickly through her hair. As she went out the talking was resumed, mixed with laughter.

She had physics next. English language was compulsory, like maths; she had picked French because it was either that or Spanish, and the choice of English literature needed no thought at all. For her last subject she had selected physics because she reckoned the homework wouldn't involve much writing. It had seemed quite a good reason at the time.

She was the first to arrive in room 21. Alsop of the grey hair came next and she smiled at him in relief; she had been wondering if she was in the wrong place. He blinked, put down his case, picked it up again and hurried out.

When he returned in the company of Sandy and Boris she kept her eyes to herself. They sat on the far side of the room. It filled up enough to prevent Polly being isolated, not enough to give her a neighbour. She was the only girl; the lecturer addressed her as Miss Devenish with a faintly solicitous note.

The last lecture of the morning was French. Polly got away smartly at the end and hurried to the canteen, buying her meal tickets from the main office on the way. She had beaten the queue and was able to pick a window table. She sat facing the view, which was over a park and quite pleasant.

'May I join you?' said a voice.

'Kim – yes, of course – do,' said Polly.

'You looked so fierce and solitary I hardly dared come over.' Quickly unloading his food he took their trays to a pile on a trolley. She was glad he didn't insist on an answer.

'What made you decide to come here?' he asked as he sat down.

'To the tech? I was fed up with school.'

'Ah, my own reason exactly. I couldn't face the sixth form – being a prefect and having to make boys wear their caps.'

Polly grinned.

'Imagine, it would have meant wearing mine. As it is I've burnt it.'

Her immediate thought was that this splendid gesture wouldn't have been possible if there were any younger brothers. She inquired.

'No; have you?'

'Two – that is three now, because of the baby. And one sister. She gets all my uniform.'

'Jolly for her.'

'She hates it. But,' said Polly thoughtfully, 'there ought to be some compensations for being the eldest.'

'Certainly there ought.' Kim swallowed some food. 'You're doing the ordinary level course, I suppose?'

'Yes. What about you?'

'A levels. French, German, Spanish.'

'Goodness.'

'Don't you fancy languages?'

'Not unless you count my own.'

'Oh, you mean English.' He seemed to shrug slightly. 'You like English?'

'Well, better than French,' said Polly, recoiling after all from the idea of sharing her recent enthusiasm for literature. She remembered she scarcely knew Kim.

They discussed the college. Talking slowed her, but made no difference to him.

'Do excuse me, won't you?' he said when he had finished.

'Of course,' said Polly, and dreamed over her pudding until his place was taken by a large raw-boned youth with a lumpy nose and bruised lips.

She filled the remaining time by going window shopping in the town. Another day she thought she might walk in the park.

The afternoon began with English language, where she expected to see Tom. He was a friend of Judith's brother, though lately he had become more Judith's friend than Mark's, just as Mark himself had become Polly's friend rather than her enemy. If it hadn't been for Tom she would probably never have thought of the technical college; though the actual suggestion had been Mark's. Tom was doing his A levels here now; he had taken the O level course last year.

Watching the door for him Polly was shocked instead by the entry of Louise. It couldn't be her. She was still at school, with Cynthia and Melody and the rest of Lower 5, or Upper 5 as they would be by this time; she was part of the past. She had no business to be here at all.

She saw Polly, waved, and sat down too far away for conversation. Sophisticated was still the word for her; even more so now that she was out of uniform. She was accompanied by several completely new faces, all girls.

A few moments later Kim came in. He glanced

round the room and went to sit by Louise. Apparently he too was one of the class.

When the lecturer turned out to be Mr. Routledge Polly was past being surprised. He had taught at her school the previous term and she had known he would be here, but hadn't expected to see him yet.

He began by taking their names.

'Liz Cartwright.'

'Short for Elizabeth?'

'I'm always called Liz.'

'Here you'll mostly be Miss Cartwright.' He wrote it down and passed on to the next.

'Maurice? Or Boris?'

'Boris, sir.'

'Boris's mum is a Russian dancer,' said Sandy.

'Thank you, Sanders.'

'Knows me,' muttered Sandy in astonishment.

'I met you on enrolment day,' said Mr. Routledge. 'You're too small to forget.'

('I nearly said "Same to you sir",' remarked Sandy afterwards. Certainly Mr. Routledge was shorter and more bristling than Polly had remembered him.)

When it came to her turn he said before she could speak: 'Devenish. Polly. Hallo.'

'Hallo sir,' said Polly.

Kim's surname was Welwyn. Of course, thought Polly.

'Kimberley? Joachim?' he was asked.

'Just Kim, sir,' he replied firmly.

Mr. Routledge didn't remember Louise at all.

When he had the last name he closed the register and stood up.

'Its,' he said.

They looked at him.

'Where's the cat?' he asked, beginning to pace in front of the desk. 'It's in its box. Who knows how the apostrophes go? Yes?'

'Well sir,' said Alsop, 'there's one between the e and the s in *where's*...'

'Mm. That wasn't the one I wanted. Wait a minute. Hands up those who don't know what an apostrophe is. No. Good. Think about it, think about it: how do they go?'

As his eye fixed them one after another they responded with different expressions; nervousness, uncertainty, in the case of Louise boredom, and from Kim the look of one who has been asked to take part in an undignified parlour game. Polly wondered how many were pretty sure of the answer but afraid to give it in case it was wrong.

'What a collection,' said Mr. Routledge. 'At least Alsop had a go.'

'Good old Dad,' said Sandy.

'Sanders?' said Mr. Routledge briskly.

'D'you want me to guess, sir?'

'Never mind. Polly?'

'The first one does and the second one doesn't, sir.' She realized she could have put it more elegantly.

He nodded and wrote it up on the board, using orange chalk for the apostrophe. 'Take it down, look at it, engrave it on your memories,' he said, writing on another part of the board *Homework: learn its.*

'You may wonder why the fuss,' he continued. 'One reason is that I've got to mark your work, and I shan't be able to keep my temper if all your itses have apostrophes where they shouldn't.'

Polly took her stiff notebook and wrote *Where's the cat? It's in its box* at the top of the first page. Alsop was getting a red pencil out of his case.

The door opened and every head turned. Tom came in.

'I'm sorry sir,' he began.

'Pleasure,' grunted Mr. Routledge.

'I didn't have the room on my timetable, sir. I thought it would be 6 same as last year but the Doctor was in there.'

'Yes. Wondered when we'd be seeing you. Have a seat.'

'Thank you sir.'

'How was the exam?'

'Oh – I failed, sir.'

'I know that.' Mr. Routledge flashed a sardonic grin at him as he faltered between two rows of desks.

Tom grinned ruefully back. 'It wasn't very nice, sir.'

'Well, you're not alone. Apart from the sorry souls who decided not to try again, there's whatsis-name come here from the grammar school especially to have a second go.' He indicated Kim, who looked slightly ruffled by this attention. 'You haven't missed much,' he continued. 'We were doing its. I'm sure you know that by now.'

'Er – I think so, sir.'

'Yes, it's on the board,' said Mr. Routledge, following Tom's hasty glance. 'Take it down if you want. I dare say you've given last year's notes to the dog.'

Polly remembered she had once felt jealous at the mere notion of Mr. Routledge teaching Tom. She hadn't realized he already was, and that his part-time job at her school was just a brief extra. He probably hadn't wanted them to know. Looking at his leather elbows and sagging jersey it was easy to believe he had needed the additional money.

She didn't join the rush for the canteen at the end of the lecture. She and Louise met on their way to the door.

'How are you getting on?' asked Louise.

'What are you doing here?' countered Polly.

Louise raised her eyebrows. Polly had always particularly disliked her when she did that. 'A secretarial course,' she said. 'They like us to come to the language lessons.'

'I didn't know you were leaving school.'

'We didn't know you were. Quite a surprise, if you remember.'

'When did you decide? After me?'

'About the same time, I believe.'

'What about your term's notice?'

'You could hardly expect Miss Hall to object in my case if she didn't in yours.'

Kim had gone on.

'See you around,' said Louise, and followed. Polly wished they hadn't spoken. She felt disproportionately enraged and would have welcomed a few words with Tom, but he had gone too.

There was a physics practical next; Polly went

slowly to the main entrance and checked the whereabouts of the lab. It was locked when she arrived. She stood in the corridor feeling thirsty and thinking of cups of tea. Presently some of the boys came and stood behind her.

'Why don't we go in?' demanded Sandy.

'You can't,' said Polly.

'Perhaps the door's locked,' said Boris.

'Yes, it is,' said Polly.

Alsop stepped forward and tried it. 'Locked,' he said.

When their lecturer of the morning appeared, Sandy said in aggrieved tones: 'Sir, we can't get in!'

'No,' replied Mr. Leigh, unlocking the door. 'I'm afraid we have to do this. There's quite a bit of valuable equipment in here – not that I'm suggesting any of you would harm it, but every college has its vandals. Anyway, it's the rule.'

'Put that monkey wrench away, Dad,' said Sandy.

'As a matter of fact we did once have the idea of labelling each object with its price. We thought it might make people more careful, but I dare say you can guess what happened.'

'They picked the expensive stuff to wreck,' said Alsop lugubriously.

Mr. Leigh looked faintly alarmed. 'Oh, er – not quite that bad. No, the labels became interchanged. Beakers were marked a hundred pounds, and on the barometer it said fourpence each.'

Sandy appeared to be wishing he had thought of this himself.

The lab was large and airy, well equipped with sinks and benches. Polly wondered if the taps contained drinking water. Mr. Leigh said today's experiment was to verify Ohm's law.

'Some of you will probably need to share.'

Polly quickly claimed a pile of apparatus; better to fumble alone than have an unwilling partner. The one lab at her school had been used regularly only by the examination classes; the nearest she had been to an experiment before was watching while Miss Saunders performed on the centre bench.

Mr. Leigh explained with the help of a diagram on the board how to connect everything up. Polly spent some seconds admiring her handful of coloured wires before selecting a red one and getting started.

Eventually everything was in place and a table had been ruled in her notebook ready for the readings. Then she found the needles on her dials were remaining obstinately at zero.

'Sir,' she said when Mr. Leigh came past, 'I can't make this work.'

'Can't you? Let's see. Perhaps you haven't got your connections tight enough.' He bent to check them and unscrewed one.

'Have you not done much practical work before, Miss Devenish?' he asked.

'No, sir.'

'No . . . well . . . what did you think this was?'

'Wire.'

'And on the outside of the wire?'

'Oh,' said Polly. 'Insulation.'

He nodded. 'You're not going to get a very good connection with that in the way, are you?'

'I suppose not, sir.'

'You need to strip the ends. Have you got a penknife? You'd better borrow mine. Like this, you see.'

Polly met an incredulous stare from Boris across the bench. She gazed haughtily back.

The practical lasted until five. As Polly dragged her case home she was working out how few books she could manage with the following day.

They were just finishing the meal when she got in.

'Here's Polly!' said Michael.

'Hallo, love,' said her mother.

Polly sat down. 'Is there a cup of tea?'

'I'll make a fresh pot.' She went to put the kettle on.

'What was it like? Was it nice?' asked Jennifer. 'Are there lots of boys in your class?'

'I haven't got a class.'

'Do you want any bacon pie?' asked Hugh.

'Yes,' said Polly, looking at the single wedge remaining on the plate.

'Oh.' Hugh went out.

'Are the boys rough? Are they like Ken?' asked Jennifer. Ken lived next door and rode a motor bike.

'No. Yes. Some of them.'

'You look tired,' said her mother, returning.

'What I need is a cup of tea.'

'Here you are. We saved some pie for you.'

'Yes, I saw. Thanks.' She drank.

'How did it go?'

'Oh, all right.'

'What are the other boys like, the ones that aren't like Ken?' asked Jennifer.

'All different.'

'Will you be getting lots of new boy friends?'

'No,' said Polly.

After a slight pause Jennifer said: 'If you don't want that pie, can I have it?'

'I do want it. Is there more tea?'

'I shouldn't wait too long to eat,' said her mother, refilling her cup, 'or you'll drown your appetite.'

'Let's go and watch television,' said Michael to Jennifer. 'We can't start our homework until Polly's off the table.'

They went out. Polly looked at the baby, who was sitting in his playpen shredding a newspaper.

'Hallo Jonathan.'

'By the way,' said her mother, 'have you any idea how the codeine got into his cot this morning?'

'I gave it him to play with. It makes a good rattle.'

'Really, Polly. You ought to have more sense.'

'But he couldn't possibly get the lid off.' She reached for the pie.

'Suppose he'd broken the bottle banging it? I don't like him having medicines, and I don't like him having anything made of glass either.'

'Oh. Sorry.'

'You won't need to do any homework this evening, will you?' said her mother in a kinder voice.

'I thought I might go round to Judith's.' She spoke without much conviction.

'I should get an early night if I were you.'

'They all have handbags,' said Polly in sudden gloom.

'Handbags? Who?'

'The girls at the tech. I should have had one instead of a case.'

'Then what would you have done with your books?'

'Oh, carried them under my arm or something. I didn't need half the ones I took today. Can I have this week's allowance in advance?'

'It won't be enough for a handbag.'

'I know, but I could get some makeup. I look awful without it.'

'Nonsense. You've got a complexion most girls would envy.'

'I look like a baby.'

'Better to look fifteen than thirty, like that little madam down the road.'

'The one Ken takes on his motorbike? She only looks about twenty. I wouldn't mind looking like her, but I need lipstick and mascara and eye shadow and —'

'You'd better see what you can afford this Friday,' interposed her mother. 'I'm not giving you money in advance for that. And remember to set something aside for tights and shoe repairs.'

'Shoe repairs,' said Polly in disgust.

2

'How are you finding the technical college?' asked Polly's father on Saturday.

She had scarcely seen him all week. He had recently become a partner in the small firm of architects he worked for, which seemed to mean longer hours.

'It's not too bad,' she said.

'Different from what you expected?'

'I can't remember what I did expect now.'

'Is the teaching good?'

'Oh yes,' said Polly, adding after a moment: 'We've got Mr. Routledge for literature and language too.'

'Is he your friend from school?'

'Yes.'

'Good,' said her father. 'Good.'

'Are you going out this afternoon, Polly?' asked her mother.

'Yes. Shopping and Garth.'

'Not Judith?'

'Judith this evening,' said Polly, confident of feeling sprightlier today than she had during the week.

Garth was better visited during the day, when his grandfather would leave them to their own devices. His mother, though anxiously friendly, never asked much; but if Polly went in the evening Mr. Mandeville either engaged them in ponderous conversation or expected them to sit quiet and listen to music.

Garth was only a boy friend when status required it: Polly's or Jennifer's. (Lately Jennifer seemed to be finding an elder sister quite an asset.) The rest of the time he was a clever fat cantankerous friend who happened to be a boy.

His house (or, as he always insisted, his grandfather's house) had a couple of large trees in the front garden; they made the short drive rather gloomy. He let her in himself, padding to the door in leather slippers. His beige sweater was expensively thin. Polly thought he would have looked better in something hairier.

'Come and see my machine,' he said, leading her up to his room.

It looked like a medieval instrument of torture. 'What is it?' asked Polly.

'A weight reducer. I've got it for a week on approval. You spend fifteen minutes a day inside it doing simple exercises. Shall I show you?'

'Yes, all right,' said Polly, crossing to his bookshelf.

'Could you just support me while I get my other leg in?' he asked breathlessly. 'Thanks. Now it just needs fastening – I wonder if you could do those buckles there.'

'How would you manage if you were on your own?'

'I can do it myself, but it takes longer. I'm not really used to it yet.' He began the exercises.

'Has your grandfather seen it?'

'My mother has. I'm trying to persuade her to pay. Luckily he wasn't in when it arrived.'

The machine creaked on.

'No new books,' she remarked conversationally.

'I have got one. I'll show you.' He disengaged an arm and wiped his forehead. 'I won't do the whole fifteen minutes now. Could you help me out?'

'Wouldn't it be simpler to dig the garden? Or go for a cross country run?'

'What ghastly ideas,' he said limply.

'I suppose they would take longer than fifteen minutes.'

'This is the book.' He opened a drawer. '*Lady Chatterley's Lover*. I borrowed it.'

'Isn't it rather hard going?' said Polly cautiously.

'A bit. But don't you want to see what all the fuss was about?'

'Yes, I suppose so. There was a short story by him I quite liked about a little boy and a rocking-horse. I haven't got very far with anything else.'

'Will your adults comment?'

They usually referred to her parents or his mother and grandfather like this. His father was dead.

Polly considered. 'I shan't bring it to their notice. Mummy didn't like me reading *1984*. She told me not to, in fact.'

'It makes me so furious!' exploded Garth. 'Why on earth shouldn't we read what we like?'

'She said it might upset me. It did,' Polly admitted. 'And I couldn't talk about it because I wasn't supposed to have read it.'

'You could have talked to me.'

'It was before I knew you.'

'That reminds me,' said Garth, 'did you know *Lollipop Boy*'s coming to the Gaumont?'

'When?'

'Two or three weeks' time, I think. I'd like to see it, but Grandfather's so bigoted about X's.'

'Well, you'll be eighteen a lot sooner than me.'

'That won't make any difference to him. Have you read any of the reviews?'

'I did read something about the boy they found for the main part, how he'd never done any acting before and it was amazing that he managed to be so good. I must say I'd quite like to see him.'

'Let's go. I'm sure you could pass as eighteen.'

'Do you think so?' Polly looked at herself in the mirror. 'Perhaps with makeup on.'

'Would you like to?'

'What would you tell your adults?'

'I needn't say what we're going to see.'

'But suppose they knew it was on?'

'Oh yes, they might.' He let the book in his hands fall open, snapped it shut, and let it open again. 'Ah,' he said. 'I could say we were going to whatever's on at the other one, the Ritz.'

'That would do for me, too. Mine mightn't mind so much if it was X for horror, but something like this . . .' Her glance fell on the leaves of his book and he quickly closed it.

'It always opens there. I think the boy who lent it to me only read that part.'

'I didn't see,' said Polly.

'Oh – well – you will if you borrow it.' He changed the subject. 'Would you like some tea?'

They went down to the kitchen.

'Isn't your mother here?'

'She's shopping. Grandfather's out as well.' He prowled round the cupboards and offered her sardines on toast.

'I'm *hungry*,' he said, attacking the tin with vigour.

'It's going sideways. Let me.'

'I didn't eat much lunch,' he explained. 'I'm trying to diet, but my mother's not very co-operative. I keep asking her to give me steak and salad, and instead she serves up roast potatoes and Yorkshire pudding and says *But you've always loved them, dear.*'

'Annoying,' agreed Polly, preoccupied with the tin.

They ate at the kitchen table. Polly had scarcely been in here before; Garth's mother usually gave them delicious snacks to balance on their laps in armchairs.

'Do you think you could show me a bit of maths some time?' she asked.

He was taken aback. 'Why me?'

'Well, because it's your thing. I mean you're good at it, and you like it.'

'You want me to try and explain some of what I'm doing?' He sounded unenthusiastic.

'No, silly, how could I understand that?'

'Well, I was wondering.'

'O level's bad enough. All I want's a bit of help with the odd things that crop up at tech.'

'Of course you're there now, aren't you.' She thought it had taken him long enough to remember. She didn't want to tell him about it if he wasn't interested, but she would have welcomed a few routine inquiries. 'Aren't the maths teachers any good?' he said.

'We call them lecturers. They're all right, it's me. I'm pretty hopeless at maths.'

He said reluctantly: 'What are these things that crop up?'

'Simultaneous equations,' replied Polly at once.

'Surely they're straightforward enough. How many unknowns?'

'Well, I'm never quite sure.'

'Are they in x and y, or x and y and z?'

She was unable to resist playing up to him a little. 'Sometimes it's a and b.'

After a moment he said: 'Have you considered changing to another subject?'

'That's an idea,' said Polly. 'Perhaps I'll try Cooking for Brides and Business Girls.' She had been charmed to find this in the prospectus.

Before the conversation could go any further Garth's mother came in laden with parcels. She was pleased to see Polly and didn't seem to object to their cooking, but it was embarrassing to watch her search for clean places to put things down amid the toast crumbs and sardine oil. Polly left soon afterwards, her offer to wash up having been refused.

She noted that maths was not something Garth was willing to share. She wondered if he considered her good enough only for life's frills. She had long suspected that he thought his mother rather silly (so did Polly sometimes, for waiting on Garth hand and foot the way she did). To his grandfather, on the other hand, he gave a grudging respect; for his maths if nothing else. Polly was a little ruffled by the conclusion she had reached; she didn't want to be lumped in with Garth's mother. Then she thought he would hardly have suggested going with his mother to *Lollipop Boy*, and grinned at the vision it conjured up.

'You look different,' said Judith.

'Oh good. I hoped you'd notice.'

'Let's see; lipstick, and . . . what?'

'Nothing,' said Polly. 'It was all I could afford this week.'

'Oh well, I shouldn't bother with anything else. That looks good; it gives you a sort of glow.'

'Really? How can it? Polly rushed to the mirror.

'I don't know, but it does. It shows off your eyes.'

'Cor.'

Judith sat down and resumed her sewing, interrupted by Polly's arrival.

'Is that the belt of your new dress?' asked Polly, watching her in the mirror.

'No, a tie.'

'A tie?' She turned round.

'For Tom.' Judith went on quickly: 'I had a bit of material left over, and it's his birthday next week.'

'Aren't ties frightfully difficult?'

'Not the sort with square ends. I got a pattern.'

'Let me have a proper look.'

'It isn't finished yet.'

'I wonder if he'll wear it?' Polly answered herself. 'Yes, it's just the kind of thing he likes. Mark wouldn't. Oh Judith, what a nice idea. Is that why you wanted to be up here?'

'Yes. Tom might come in downstairs, and even if he didn't I'd rather Mark didn't see.'

'Yes, I suppose he might tease.'

'I wasn't quite sure you wouldn't.'

'Would I be so mean?'

'Yes.'

'Oh. Well, perhaps you're right.' She sat down on the stool and rested her elbows on her knees, watching Judith. 'I haven't seen very much of Tom at tech so far. He keeps dashing off.'

'I expect you make him nervous.'

'I seem to make them all nervous. The boys, I mean.'

'Not really? I was joking. Have you seen Louise?'

'Yes I have,' said Polly indignantly. 'Did you know she was going to be there?'

'Not until Cynthia told us this term. She seemed a bit disgruntled; I don't think she'd known very long herself. Batty reckons Louise was afraid of starting a stampede.'

'Well she might be. I'm sure she only thought of it because I was going. Or else it was because of Kim. And then she had the cheek to say I was doing it because of Mr. Routledge!'

'How did you know that?'

'Melody told me.'

'English lessons are very different now we're back to Miss Crispian. Batty and I quite miss him, but nobody else does.'

And what's school like without me, Polly wondered. She realized she had been half hoping Judith would say that it was awful and she wished Polly hadn't left; in which case she just might have admitted that so did she. What she hadn't expected at all were the comfortable references to Penelope Batts. She had for a long time vaguely considered Batty as her own reserve friend, who might be cultivated one day if she got round to it. Batty had once confided that she kept a model village and made up stories about its imaginary inhabitants; she had even said Polly could see it.

'Did you know Kim was at tech too?' she asked.

'Louise's Kim?' Judith was surprised.

'He isn't that much hers. He talks to all the girls; the canteen ladies call him Romeo.' ("Come on, Romeo," one had said, and he had replied "I'm glad to see you recognize me.") 'He's taking language again, like Tom, and doing A levels – French and German and Spanish. He wants to get a degree in modern languages and then a job in the Foreign Office.'

'Very nicely mapped out.'

'Don't you think he'll manage it?'

'Failing English doesn't seem a brilliant beginning.'

'I think he's very peeved about that, though he doesn't say so. He doesn't like coming to Mr. Routledge's lectures much. Nor does Louise. I wish she wouldn't, she doesn't really have to.'

'Perhaps she feels like the occasional O level to garnish her shorthand. You still enjoy Mr. Routledge though, I hope?'

'Oh yes. And the literature's lovely – it's so restful, nobody takes it, and it's in a funny little classroom like a box —'

'Nobody?' said Judith with raised eyebrows.

'Nobody noticeable. Not Liz, or Sandy or Boris or Dad, or Louise of course, or Kim.'

What strange names.'

'Dad is Alsop. His hair is grey in front. Sandy is Sanders, and Boris's mum is a Russian dancer.' Polly had made herself giggle, but seeing Judith at a loss she continued quickly: 'Liz is a loud sort of girl. She overflows. She's fallen for one of the maths lecturers and she keeps saying how sweet he is.'

'Is he?'

'Norris?' Polly wrinkled her nose. 'No, he's a twerp. I should think this is his first job. He's all pink and woffly, and he calls the boys mister.'

'You make me feel quite sorry for him.' Judith put her needle away.

'Like Liz. I say, is that the tie finished?'

'Except for pressing.' She laid the strip of bright material over her knees and smoothed it with one finger.

'Let's do it now, then you could try it on with your school blouse.'

They went downstairs and Judith got out a gleaming iron, bought by her mother only the day before. 'The old one had been failing for some time.'

'Poor thing.'

'It's never really been the same since the day Mark thought he could dry a pair of thick nylon socks in a hurry by ironing them.'

'I shouldn't think the socks have either. Does Batty still wear socks?'

'Black stockings, this term. A definite improvement. She is a surprising person; do you know she's built a whole model village in her room at home?'

'I did know actually.'

'It's got houses and shops and a church and everything. It covers half the floor; her mother just lets it stay there.'

'You've seen it, have you?'

'Yes, I went to tea one day.' She broke off at the sound of a door, and whisked the tie upstairs as Mark came in.

'Polly! Hallo. How's the tech?'

'Tiring.'

'Oh, has Judith been trying the new iron? I must have a go.'

'Do you know how to work it?' asked Polly seriously.

'I'm very handy at ironing. I sometimes do myself a shirt when Ma's in the middle of a book.' He looked among the clean washing and found some teacloths. 'I suppose going on until five each day must be rather exhausting. Do you like it otherwise though?'

He sounded quite anxious. 'Yes,' said Polly. It was at least half true, and she didn't want him feeling guilty on her behalf. 'Yes,' she repeated after a longish pause, 'it's fun. You're scorching that.'

'So I am. A lot less discipline, is there?'

'Well, we can't smoke.'

'Do you want to?'

'No, not at all.' She grinned. 'Apart from that it's

very free. We dance in the lunch break. People do, I mean. I haven't yet.'

'I don't know much about dancing.'

'You couldn't know less than me.'

Judith came back and started to make coffee.

'I say, the new iron's marvellous,' Mark told her. 'It keeps on scorching these teacloths.'

'Turn it down, then!'

'Why? They're linen. It's on linen.'

'They must be too dry. Here, let me finish them, you're not safe; you do the coffee.'

He did the coffee, and Polly talked about the technical college until it was time for her to go.

3

'Ow,' said Liz. 'What a meal. That treacle roll's finished me.'

'Not much good for anyone trying to diet,' said Polly.

'Aren't you trying to diet?' Liz made eyes of amazement. 'You must be the only person I know who isn't.'

'I've never thought about it.'

'Well no, I suppose you've no need.' Polly said nothing. She didn't think dieting would change Liz much either; she was designed to be large.

'Coming dancing, Liz?' asked another girl.

'Can't. I'm too stodged. And I've got Routledge's homework to do,' she added as they went upstairs.

'I've got Norris's,' said Polly.

'Oh, I did that last night. I wish he taught us something with a bit more soul. How can you convey your feelings in a page of trigonometry?'

'How could you in anything else? Watch out!'

There was a clatter on the stairs and Liz lurched sideways, grabbing at Polly for support.

'Er – Miss Cartwright,' said Dr. Makepiece from behind, 'I think you've dropped your heel.'

'Damn! I mean thank you sir.'

She sat down on the top step and searched in her handbag. 'Do you think he heard what we were saying?' Taking out a tube of Seccotine she applied it to the heel and clapped it back on the shoe.

'I shouldn't think so. How efficient!'

'Practice. I'd better not wear it yet, do you mind if I hop?'

'Have my arm.'

'Anyway, what the hell,' said Liz as they proceeded jerkily down the corridor, 'it never came in his speech. *The girls are not to become unduly fond of the lecturers.*'

'*Nor are the boys.*'

'Polly!'

Room 24 was empty except for three or four of the girls. They often spent the lunch hour in the place where their first afternoon lecture would be. Liz waved her shoe and told what had happened. 'And there was the Doctor, as large as life.'

Polly settled herself and frowned over Mr. Norris's maths. No good asking Liz for help; hers, though beautifully written, would as likely as not be nonsense. It was taken for granted that all their textbooks had answers, which meant one was under a kind of moral pressure to work things out twice (Polly drew the line at twice) rather than give in stuff one knew to be wrong.

'Bordigals,' she muttered.

'What?' said Liz.

'Nothing.'

'It sounded dreadful. What does it mean?'

'Something dreadful.'

'Well, go on. What?'

'I don't know. I invented it.'

'*Oh!*'

Presently the girls began making up their faces in readiness for the afternoon. Polly propped her case open in front of her.

'Oh look. I say, isn't that clever,' said Liz.

Inside the lid Polly had fixed a small mirror and a pocket to hold her comb and lipstick. The others looked and admired.

'Damn it, my lashes won't stay on,' muttered Liz.

'You are falling to bits today.' Polly instantly wondered if she had gone too far, and was relieved when Liz laughed.

'Now they've come off again! Well, I can't be bothered with them. They'll just have to stay off.' She bundled them roughly into her handbag as though it was their fault. She looked quite different without them; easier to like, thought Polly, strolling over to the window.

The boys began to come in, bringing noise and cold air and knocking a magazine from Liz's table in passing. Sandy read from it as he picked it up.

'"Handy hint: I boil all my odd stockings in a little water for fifteen minutes."'

'After this,' said Polly, 'they look so odd I don't mind throwing them away.'

He gave her a surprised grin and she returned to her seat, having just seen Kim walking alone up the hill.

Sandy and Boris sat in their usual place in front of Dad.

'Done the Doctor's homework?'

'I tried,' said Dad.

There was an empty chair next to Polly. Kim took it when he arrived.

'Now for my favourite rest cure,' he said, leaning back and crossing his legs.

'Rest cure?'

'One only has to listen to old Routledge twenty per cent of the time, don't you find? The rest is repetition.'

'That's why it's a rest cure,' said Tom, who had followed him in.

'I hope you choose the right twenty per cent,' said Polly. 'Hallo,' she added to Tom. 'Many happy returns of yesterday.'

'Thanks.'

'But you're not wearing it!'

Tom blushed slightly and put an involuntary hand to his throat. 'Two chaps were having stew in the canteen the other day,' he said without preliminary, 'and one said to the other "This is revolting. I'm just about at the end of my tether." So the other said "Oh, do you eat the tether?"'

Polly groaned.

'Where does he get them from?' said Kim.

Tom looked bashful and passed on. Louise came in with two of her fellow secretaries, glanced at Kim and sat at the back of the room. It was Mr. Routledge's term for them; 'The secretaries needn't do this if they don't want,' he sometimes said of the homework, or he might write on the board 'HWK FOR ALL, PARTIC. SECS.'

'He's late,' said Polly.

'He always is.'

She was annoyed with herself. She didn't want to discuss Mr. Routledge with Kim, and had only spoken at all because of his air of waiting to be entertained. 'The Doctor comes in punctual to the second. I suppose you don't have him.'

'Doctor Makepiece? No.'

'Who do you have?' Heavens, how dull.

'Smith, Wright and Stevenson.'

'We have Stevenson. For French. Oh, here he comes.'

Mr. Routledge banged his briefcase down on the table and took out a pile of paper. 'Test,' he said, dealing it rapidly round the class. A flutter of resignation followed him.

Polly wrote briskly. When the questions were hard it wasn't the kind of hardness that would yield to extra time. She finished first, leaving some blanks, and watched the others. Kim worked in a leisurely fashion with occasional pauses for thought. Liz groaned; Sandy screwed his little finger into his ear. Dad shook his pen, depressed the lever and let it creak slowly back, whispered to Sandy and Boris, and leaned across to Louise, who shook her head.

'Won't she help you?' asked Mr. Routledge sympathetically. 'After you carried her case all the way from the bus stop too!'

Dad went red and Louise gazed into space with a little frown at the top of her nose.

'Borrow your ink?' asked Sandy, appearing suddenly at Polly's side.

'Sanders, stop bouncing about like a tiddlywink.'

'Tiddlywink,' echoed Dad with approval.

Polly gave Sandy her ink to pass on.

'Who by having any more time could do any

more good?' asked Mr. Routledge. There was no reply. 'Right, change papers.'

Polly changed with Kim. Some of his answers were flowery versions of what was required, difficult to mark precisely. She gave him the benefit of the doubt, and still found when they changed back that she had done better than him.

'I'm sure you could beat me into the ground if you really tried,' he murmured pleasantly.

Mr. Routledge took the marks in. Polly was near the top. It was odd; English language was rules with him just as it had been with Miss Crispian – no writing the life history of a penny, or what she did in the holidays – yet suddenly she could manage it. Indeed, she didn't see how anyone could not: how Liz, for instance, could wail with dismay time and again because she had forgotten *its*.

At the end of the lecture Louise paused on her way out.

'Coming for a cup of tea?' said Kim.

'I feel more like coffee.' She added carelessly: 'The Begonia's just across the road.'

'You could pop over,' said Kim.

'I could.' Her glittering smile included Polly for a moment, and then she was gone.

Kim accompanied Polly to the canteen. The queue was out of the door when they arrived.

'Look here, you go and sit down. I'll bring your tea.'

She did as he said and then wished she hadn't; she felt silly, alone at a bare table.

'No tea?' said Tom, joining her.

'Kim's getting it.'

He leaned closer. 'Have you seen the tie Judith gave me?'

'Yes, I watched her making it.'

'She's good at making things, isn't she.'

'She always has been. I'm sorry I brought it up like that just now.'

'Oh, I didn't mind.'

Sandy, Boris and Dad came over and pulled up an extra chair. By the time Kim arrived there was nowhere for him to sit and scarcely room for his cup on the table. Polly took hers in an awkward silence, even Sandy being dumbfounded by Kim's chivalry, and fumbled for her purse.

'You're having it on me,' said Kim, grabbing a free chair and drawing himself in between her and Tom.

'Oh, well, thank you.'

'A pleasure. Do you smoke?'

'No, we aren't allowed.'

'Good heavens yes, I remember hearing about that.'

'I wouldn't anyway. Too expensive.'

'How right you are,' sighed Kim, lighting his own and pushing the matchbox across to Tom. 'There you are, a joke for your collection.'

'Read it out,' said Sandy, but Tom wouldn't. Polly took the box herself and laid out matches for a puzzle.

'Oh not one of them,' said Sandy, rolling his eyes in dismay.

Kim leaned forward calmly and moved the allowed number of matches to give the solution.

'Anyone know a cure for warts?' asked Dad.

'Why,' said Sandy, 'doesn't she love you warts and all?'

'Oh shut up. I only wanted to borrow her ink, if she'd had any. And I didn't carry her case; I was just walking up with her when Routledge saw us.'

'He probably thought you should've,' said Boris.

'Let's see.' Sandy grabbed Dad's hand. 'Cor yes. I'll charm them for you if you like.'

'Do you know how?'

'Forty pressups every day, and your wart will go away.'

Dad said: 'I've got more than one.'

'It's better to cure one at a time by this method. Not many people can do eighty pressups a day.'

'Or a hundred and twenty,' murmured Boris.

'I might manage half a dozen,' offered Dad.

'Forty for warty,' said Sandy firmly.

Tom laughed.

'Have you got warts?' Sandy asked him. 'Oh yes, look; there's one on your thumb.'

'So there is,' said Tom humbly.

'They cure a wart in *Tom Sawyer*,' said Polly. 'What is it they do?' Kim shook his head. 'Tie a bit of cotton round and then pull? . . . no, of course, that's the loose tooth.'

'Of course,' said Kim.

Sandy jumped up and announced that he was getting something to eat.

'Mind my tea, tiddlywink,' said Boris.

'Tiddlywink! He might have called me a squib.'

'Is there much difference?' asked Kim.

Polly felt strained. It was almost a relief to get away from the canteen.

'I didn't sit with you because I thought you'd rather have Gorgeous to yourself,' said Liz.

'It didn't quite work out like that.'

'Oh well, you put snotty Louise's nose out of joint anyway.'

'Do you think I did?' said Polly with satisfaction.

Mr. Norris came in, sat down and began calling the register. He was one of the few lecturers who never forgot.

'. . . Mr. Alsop . . . Mr. Brown . . . Miss Cartwright . . .'

'What are you laughing at, Mr. Sanders?' asked Dad.

'The same as you, Mr. Alsop!' replied Sandy smartly.

'Sssh!' said Liz. She didn't at all mind playing the elder sister at times.

'I'll take your homework in now,' said Mr. Norris, going round the room in large brown shoes that squeaked. His brown trousers had turnups and his hair was cut very short. Liz leaned over the table with hers and Polly's. 'Thank you, Miss Cartwright,' he said.

He didn't thank the boys. Some of them kept him waiting while they searched among their books and papers.

'Did we have any, sir?' asked Sandy.

'What's that?'

'I didn't think we had any, sir.'

'Yes you did,' said Mr. Norris, standing straighter. 'You had numbers ten to fifteen on page 5, exercise 3 – I mean, sorry, page 3, exercise 5 —'

'Oh yes sir,' said Sandy. 'I've found it now, sir.'

Mr. Routledge usually got them to leave it as they went out at the end; 'homework on the corner,' he would say, standing to light a reflective cigarette.

Mr. Norris went to the board and began teaching them something new. He wrote fast, glancing frequently at the notes on his table. Occasionally he paused for a moment to invite questions. Liz responded at once.

'Which bit don't you follow, Miss Cartwright?' he asked anxiously.

'All of it really.'

'Oh. Oh, I see. Does anyone else feel like that?'

Nobody answered. If they were the same as Polly they were too stupefied to care.

'Well, naturally it needs a little time to sink in. I think the best thing would be for you to go through it after you've taken it down, and if it still bothers you give me a call.'

On the next occasion she was precise. 'I don't see how you get that A, sir, four lines from the top in the middle.'

'Oh,' he said, 'well . . . there isn't really anything to see about that.'

After a while he looked at his watch and set them some examples to do. Polly, doodling on a piece of rough paper, drew a face with a look of Kim. She was impressed; she could never have done it if she'd been trying. She folded the paper and tucked it inside her book.

'What's sec, sir?' asked Boris, leafing through his tables.

'I beg your pardon?' said Mr. Norris, startled. There were snorts of laughter and his colour rose.

'I mean,' said Boris patiently, 'what's the sec of an angle, sir?'

'It's one over cos. You ought to know that. I gave it you in your notes.'

'Thanks, sir.'

Mr. Norris was marking their homework as he sat.

'Come here a minute, Mr. Sanders.' Sandy bounced out. 'Can you explain what you were trying to do here?'

Sandy made a face at them over the lecturer's head. 'Well, sir . . .' he began.

It was Liz next. In her enthusiasm she nearly knocked over a chair.

'It seems rather a strange method, Miss Cartwright, and you haven't used it anywhere else . . .'

'Oh, I was just trying everything I could think of – I was trying everything I could think of, sir.'

Returning to her place she muttered to Polly: 'I *can't* call him sir. It would be so much easier to say sugar or honey bunch.'

'You would make him blush.'

Mr. Norris looked at his watch and then at the clock. 'That's slow, isn't it?' he exclaimed, jumping up. 'I shall be running into Dr. Makepiece's time in a moment. Never mind about the homework, I'll set you some next time.' He was gone.

'Seemed a bit upset,' said Dad.

'Left his pen,' observed Boris.

'I'll run after him,' said Liz, but before she could stir Dr. Makepiece came in.

'Good afternoon, everybody. Davis, please will you collect the homework? Let's see, it was numbers one, two and three, wasn't it? Any difficulties? Alsop?'

'Yes sir,' said Dad, 'number one.'

'Anything else?'

'Yes sir,' said Dad, 'two and three.'

'Dear me.' He took a pile of rough paper and went to sit beside him half-way down the room.

A shadow appeared beyond the frosted glass panel of the door. It vanished and reappeared; became a blur of pink, swam into features with a flattened nose in their centre. The viewer was more visible to them than they must be to him.

The door opened. Mr. Norris glanced in, squeaked across to the table and took his pen. They watched in silence, mesmerized, as he started to squeak out again.

'It's a pleasure Mr. Norris!' said Dr. Makepiece loudly.

'Oh Dr. Makepiece I'm so sorry – I didn't see you sitting there—' He dropped the pen in his agitation. Through the laughter Liz could be heard saying clearly that it was a shame.

'It was!' she said afterwards. 'It was rotten of the Doctor.'

'I suppose he couldn't resist it.'

On the steps outside the main entrance they found Kim.

'Hallo!' said Liz, pleased at the prospect of extra company on the way down the hill.

'Good night,' he replied absently, watching the doors behind them.

'One in the eye for us,' said Liz as soon as they were out of earshot.

'Um . . . I think Norris should grow his hair, don't you?'

'And hide the back of his dear little neck?' cried Liz, successfully diverted from turning her head. Polly, hurrying along, didn't want to be told that Kim was following with Louise.

At the end of her road she encountered her father.

'You're rather late home,' he said.

'Tech doesn't finish until five.'

'Of course.'

'Aren't you rather early?'

'Yes, I suppose I am.'

They walked in an easy silence, gently swinging their cases as they passed gardens bright with dahlias and chrysanthemums. Their own garden had dead leaves on the grass and a few late roses climbing over the summerhouse.

'Both of you together? That's good,' said Mrs. Devenish. 'Are you very hungry?'

Polly's father said he would make omelettes. He didn't usually cook for anyone but himself. Polly laid two places, and on his instructions put some limp rolls in the oven to crisp. They ate at the kitchen table while Jennifer and Hugh washed the tea things. They both had books, but Polly was distracted from hers by the memory of something Mr. Routledge had said the term before, at school. 'Do you do any writing?' he'd asked, and when she'd said she didn't: 'Not even a diary, a girl of your age?' She thought she was beginning to see the attraction of diaries.

She had bought a number of stiff-covered notebooks at the beginning of term, and on discovering how heavy they were had made each do for pairs of subjects occurring on the same day. This left several notebooks in hand. After her meal she selected one and sat down in front of it, paralysed at first by the clean empty page. Once she started writing she went on until interrupted by the telephone. The younger ones stampeded to answer it and Jennifer called 'Polly, it's a boy for you!' Jerked out of one dream into another, she ran.

'Polly? I thought you were coming round this evening.'

'Garth. Hallo. Did I say, yes I did, didn't I. I'm afraid I've got an awful lot of homework this evening actually.'

'Oh.'

'You could come here if you liked.'

'Well. If you've got to work, there doesn't seem much point.' She had expected the refusal; he found her family rather overwhelming.

'How's your machine?' she asked.

'I sent it back.'

'Ah.'

'Decided it was a swindle.'

'Um.' She had had to break off in the middle of a sentence and was afraid of forgetting how it ended.

'Remember *Lollipop Boy* next Saturday, won't you?'

'Goodness, is that when it is? Thanks for reminding me.' She said good-bye and rang off quickly, hurrying back to her book.

'Are you writing poetry?' asked Jennifer.

'What? Of course not.' Polly shielded the page.

'Sarah's sister writes poetry.'

'Nice for Sarah.'

'She lets her read it sometimes. What are you writing if it isn't poetry?'

'A story.' ('Nothing to stop you writing stories,' Mr. Routledge had said.)

'A story! Oh Polly, let me see. Will you read it to us? Is it like the ones you used to tell?'

'No. It's private,' she said shortly, putting it aside.

Jennifer had spoiled her mood; her enthusiasm for the lie was somehow upsetting. Polly opened her case and dragged out her books. It was true about her homework.

4

'Can I have Liz to tea this Saturday?' asked Polly.

'Liz? Is she the one who wears the wig?'

'No, just false eyelashes.'

'Do you want to?'

'Yes.'

'You'll have to help tidy up before she comes.'

'Oh, Liz won't care.'

'I shall, though,' said Mrs. Devenish sharply. 'I'm not having anyone see the house in its present state.'

'I haven't got to do the whole house, have I?'

'Not the *whole* house, no, of course not. You might start by clearing the sideboard, and your end of the windowsill. I don't know when I was last able to dust either of those.'

'Oh, but that's where I keep my tech books. Can't I? They're in one tidy pile. I haven't got anywhere else to put them, and they're handy when I'm working at the table.'

'If I say yes to you it'll only encourage the others.'

'They couldn't be any worse. Theirs isn't stuff they need, though.'

'Well,' said Mrs. Devenish reluctantly, 'if you really haven't got anywhere else. But remember that window's inclined to leak in heavy rain.'

'Oh good, thanks. I'm sure it hardly ever leaks, it hasn't for ages. And I'll ask Liz tomorrow.'

Liz accepted with pleasure, and dressed for the occasion in a tight skirt and a billowing blouse. Her heels were rather high and her hair was all on top of her head. The general effect was best described by Hugh, who got a savage dig from Polly for muttering 'She looks topply.' Liz paid no attention; she had just caught sight of Jonathan.

'A baby! Polly, you never said!'

'I didn't know you liked them.'

'Oh yes. Oh he's a perfect pet. Children are the end, but I adore babies. Shake hands, then?' She gave him a finger, blithely unaware that her audience included the other three younger members of Polly's family. Hugh walked out in disgust; he had been the baby until Jonathan came, and certainly didn't adore him. Michael grew pink with multiple embarrassment and Jennifer, though a year younger, firmly excluded herself from Liz's statement by saying in her best social manner: 'They are awful, aren't they? Particularly little boys.' She had put on her prettiest dress for the afternoon, and had been scandalized by Polly's failure to change out of casual Saturday wear.

'Baby boys are gorgeous though,' said Liz, belatedly diplomatic, 'aren't they, you darling?'

'Would you like to hold him?' offered Jennifer, coming forward.

'No, leave him alone,' Polly told her, 'you can't hand him round like a parcel.'

'It would be taking a liberty, wouldn't it, precious? What's his name?'

'Jonathan, and I'm Jennifer.'

'And that's Michael,' said Polly.

'Hallo Jonathan, can I come in?' Kicking off her shoes, Liz climbed over the side of the playpen. Jonathan looked astounded. She tried his rattles, squeaked his squeaking dog, and built his rubber baby shapes into a tower. He reached out, interested, and managed to knock it down. She rebuilt it four times, and then began searching her handbag for possible toys.

'Why can't we have tea now she's here?' said the voice of Hugh from the kitchen. Polly thought it wasn't a bad idea and went to see.

'The icing on the cake's still sticky,' said her mother. 'I suppose you could begin laying the table if you want.'

'Have you iced it? Cor, what luxury.'

'We do our best.' Mrs. Devenish untied her apron. 'I'll be in in a minute to say hallo; I must comb my hair.'

Liz was still sharing the playpen when she entered.

'Oh Mrs. Devenish, I hope you don't mind.'

'No . . . not at all,' was the astonished answer, but Liz was already leaping out to the sound of ripped cloth.

'Hell and damnation!' she cried.

'It wasn't your skirt,' said Polly.

'Oh, then it must have been my slip. That's in shreds already.'

Jonathan stayed on the floor during tea.

'I suppose he's too small to know we're eating,' said Liz, gazing over her shoulder.

'Can I give him a biscuit?' asked Jennifer.

'No,' said Mrs. Devenish, glad it wasn't Liz who'd asked. 'If he cries he can have a rusk. What's he playing with, a comb? Where did he get that?'

'It's mine,' said Liz. 'It's quite clean, at least I hope so.'

Jonathan banged everything within reach with the comb and then started sucking it. Polly wondered if her father would come in; she thought it would probably be better if he didn't, he never knew what to say to her friends.

'Do you like the technical college?' Mrs. Devenish asked Liz.

'Oh it's terrific. We've got some lovely lecturers.'

'I'm going there when I'm fifteen,' said Jennifer.

'First I've heard of it,' said Polly.

'We'll have to see,' said Mrs. Devenish temperately.

'Why will we? If Polly can why can't I?'

'Fancy wanting to be the same as Polly,' said Hugh.

Michael hastily pushed what remained on his plate into his mouth and asked for a piece of cake. Mrs. Devenish cut it and passed it round. Liz ate three pieces.

'I can't help it,' she said sadly, 'it's so delicious.'

'I'll clear out now, and wash up later if that's all right,' said Polly, whose turn it was.

'I think we should do it all now,' said Jennifer, imagining her half of the job might well be taken over by Liz if they did; but her mother sided with Polly, and the two older girls went off upstairs as soon as the table was finished.

'What about your homework?' said Mrs. Devenish as Jennifer wandered aimlessly through the house. 'You don't want to leave it all for tomorrow.'

'I haven't got much.' She slowly mounted the stairs.

'You look easily eighteen,' said the voice of Liz through the bedroom door. She went in. Polly and Liz were crouched in front of the piece of mirror; Liz had her handbag open and the bed was strewn with makeup of various kinds.

'What are you doing?' asked Jennifer unnecessarily.

'Mind your own,' said Polly without turning her head.

'Can I put some on?'

Polly clenched her teeth and continued to apply liquid eyeliner. 'Your mother mightn't like it,' said Liz.

'She wouldn't mind.'

Polly's hand slipped and she swung round abruptly. 'Go away. Look what you've made me do,' she said. 'And you know perfectly well Mummy would be furious.'

'Sarah's sister lets her use hers.'

'Then Sarah must look ridiculous.'

'Not half as ridiculous as you. I could do much better than that if you'd let me have a try.' She turned to Liz. 'Can't I?'

'No!' said Polly. 'Go away and leave us alone!'

'I shan't. This is my room as well.' She arranged herself on her bed with her back to the wall.

'I'll get Mummy to make you.'

'Go on then, if you want her to see you like that.'

Jennifer smoothed her dress. Polly, on her way to the door, checked and came back.

'Your mother doesn't mind for you, does she?' said Liz curiously.

'She's a bit funny about it. I don't think I will go down.'

'Knew you wouldn't,' said Jennifer.

'Pay no attention,' advised Liz. 'That's what I do with James and Rob.'

'You're lucky not to have a sister. I suppose it means you've got a room to yourself?'

'If you can call it a room. It's more of a cupboard really.'

'Still, your own place; it must be nice.'

'Oh yes. I think I'd go mad sometimes if I couldn't get by myself for a bit.'

'I think I shall go mad.'

'Perhaps you could build a partition in here – no, not with the window where it is.'

Jennifer got up and went out.

'She can ask whosit's sister to let her have a go,' said Liz. 'Let's see; your left eye could do with a bit more green, I think.' They bent to the mirror again.

'Can I really borrow all this for *Lollipop Boy*?'

'Sure. I've got two of everything. At least two,' she amended, surveying the scatter on the bed. 'I like variety.' She took down her hair and began to brush it.

'You really are lucky not having a sister. Jennifer's always been more of a pest than the boys. Hugh's awful, but it's the sort of awful I can manage; and Michael just hates trouble.'

'Oh well – family.' Liz looked at her reflection. 'I think I'll change the colour of my hair soon. I'm getting a bit fed up with rose mahogany.'

'What are you really?'

'Sort of mud, I think. I can hardly remember.' She grimaced. 'I warn you, don't start on rinses. You'll never be able to stop. It looks so awful when it's growing out; you simply have to have another.' She plunged her hands into the dark silky mass. 'French loaf, I think,' she decided, and began rolling it rapidly into shape.

'Perhaps I'll grow mine. Did it take long?'

'Not very. You know what, you ought to come dancing one lunch. You never do.'

Polly was taken aback by the change of subject. 'I can't dance.'

'There's nothing to it. Just move in time to the music. Haven't you ever tried?'

'Not really.' It had been Louise's set who danced in the school gym; Polly and Judith had considered themselves above such antics.

'Come downstairs and try now. Or can we bring the radio up here?'

Polly fetched it, meeting nobody but Michael on the way. Liz found a suitable station and advised Polly to remove her shoes.

'Hold my hands to start with; it'll help you get the feel. I used to dance with the doorhandle at home. My mother got cross because it kept coming off.'

Polly quickly found it as easy as Liz had said. She seemed to be part of the music; it was an exhilarating sensation. They grew wilder and wilder, and didn't even hear when Jennifer opened the door.

'Daddy says what on earth are you doing, you'll bring the ceiling down!'

'Oh,' said Polly.

Liz switched off the radio and looked at her watch. 'I ought to go. It's been fun; I'll fix with my mother when I can have you back.'

A little later Polly cleaned her face and thought about privacy. The trouble was the house was too small. There was nowhere to bolt to unless you counted the landing cupboard. Or the loft.

She went outside her room and looked up at the trapdoor which led to the loft. There ought to be a ladder in the cupboard; there was. She placed it in position and began to climb. The trapdoor seemed immovable until she noticed that it had hinges, and applied her strength accordingly. It went up all of a sudden, and cold dusty air rushed out.

She put her head through the hole. The loft wasn't completely dark; it had a pane of perspex set into the tiles half-way along. As her eyes accustomed themselves to the dimness she saw that it was vast. The cobwebbed rafters went up and up; the joists stretched the length of the house. After a few moments she pulled herself inside and sat on the edge of the hole.

It seemed a bit feeble to go no farther. The joists looked strong, though she was pretty sure it would be disastrous to tread between them. As she didn't trust her balance she crawled. There was a tank with a platform round it where she stood to rest her knees, getting a shock when water suddenly began to gurgle and hammer inside the metal walls. She realized somebody must have turned on a tap, and decided to go back as soon as her heart had stopped jumping. As she went she heard the discovery of the ladder. The voices sounded odd from up here.

'Oh look, Daddy's in the loft.'

'What on earth . . . I thought he was downstairs. John?'

'It's me,' said Polly, feeling with her feet for the top rung.

'Polly! Who said you could go up there?'

'Nobody said I couldn't.' She closed the trapdoor and climbed down.

'Nobody thought you'd try. Just look at your clothes!'

'It'll brush off.'

'Yes, well not all over the landing, please. Go outside the back door.'

Polly went.

'I've just been making clear to the younger ones that the loft is out of bounds,' said her mother when she came in. 'I wish you wouldn't do things like that. You might easily have put a foot through the plaster.'

'I was careful.'

'Good heavens.' Her mother looked more closely at her face. 'Jennifer wasn't exaggerating.'

'What about? It doesn't show. I cleaned it off.'

'Yes, I can see you tried.'

Polly was reminded of her need for privacy. 'The loft's huge, isn't it? It seems silly to waste all that space.'

'We use it for storage sometimes.'

'I was thinking, couldn't we turn it into a room?'

'Of course not. How?'

'It would need a bit doing to it – we'd have to put in a bigger window and some floorboards, but I'm sure Daddy could manage that easily. I'd help.'

'Don't be absurd, Polly, he wouldn't even try.'

'Why not? He's an architect. And he made the summer house.'

'You can ask him if you like. I know what his answer will be.'

'But I do so need a room of my own!'

'It would be nice,' agreed her mother.

'What, me in the loft?'

'No no, that's a ridiculous idea. I meant if you could have a proper room to yourself.'

'Well I can't, can I,' said Polly, disgruntled.

'You could, perhaps, if we moved to a larger house.'

'*Moved?* Are we going to?'

'Daddy and I have been thinking about it. Don't say anything to the younger ones.'

'Could we afford?'

'We might be able to.'

Polly was thoughtfully silent.

'It's very far from being definite,' said her mother hastily.

'We've always lived here,' said Polly.

'Yes, I feel a bit like that.'

'Liz has a room to herself, she says, but small... Judith's is a good size.'

'Liz is very different from Judith, isn't she.'

'That's why I like her.'

Mrs. Devenish said in slightly troubled tones: 'I

hope you don't feel Judith should have gone to the tech just to keep you company.'

'Of course not, but nobody wants their friends to be all alike. I say – you know that cheap offer for a handyman book that came for Daddy last week; what d'you think he's done with it?'

'Thrown it away, I expect. Or if he hasn't I have.'

'Oh,' said Polly; and at her earliest opportunity she went through the rubbish box. She was too attached to her inspiration for the loft to let it go without any struggle at all.

'What are you doing?' asked Hugh.

'What do you think?'

'My little red racing car!' He pounced. 'Who threw that away?'

'Oh Hugh, you can't possibly have wanted it,' said Mrs. Devenish, coming in. 'Its wheels are gone and it's all nasty sharp edges; it isn't even red any more. Polly, what a mess. Put it all back at once before everyone comes and starts ferreting.'

'But it's the first car I ever had!' Hugh was outraged.

'Keep it out of the way, then. I don't want Jonathan getting hold of it, he could cut himself.'

Polly had found what she was looking for. As she had thought, it was possible to get the book for ten days on approval. She made a furtive telephone call to Judith and got permission to use her address before sending off the card. It didn't even need a stamp.

5

'Your compendium of do-it-yourself has arrived,' said Judith on the telephone next Saturday. 'Will you collect it this afternoon?'

'Right. Oh no, bother, I told Garth I'd go round.' They hadn't completed the arrangements for *Lollipop Boy*; Garth had been reluctant to do so over the telephone, but now it had come to the actual day it couldn't be put off any more. 'Still, I needn't stay very long, I suppose.'

'Or you could bring Garth with you.'

'Oh – could I? Well, I'll see.'

Garth was sweeping up leaves in the drive when she arrived.

'That'll do your weight good,' said Polly.

He looked at her suspiciously, resting on his broom. 'Grandfather's orders.'

'I'll move the piles. Is that what the hod's for? Where are you putting them?'

'Round behind the garage. I'm supposed to burn them.'

'Oh, a bonfire! Can I light it now?'

He passed her the matches, and went on sweeping slowly until she returned.

'It's burning. I must hurry and take some more.'

'We're all right with the other film tonight,' he said, not increasing his pace. 'The one at the Ritz.'

'It's a war escape thing, isn't it? I noticed it was a U.'

'*Courage By Night*. You'd better know the name if that's what we're supposed to be going to see. Where shall we meet?'

'Outside the cinema, I thought?'

'Right. It begins at eight. I've told my adults I'm going with you, so if they mention it just remember it's *Courage By Night* we're going to see.'

'I won't come inside actually, so you needn't worry.'

'You won't come inside?' he repeated, stopping again to lean on his broom.

'There's no point now we've fixed things up. And I'm supposed to be going round to Judith's.'

'I thought you'd be staying to tea. My mother's made a cake.'

Polly knew quite well his mother was always making cakes. She hadn't intended to repeat Judith's invitation, but it wouldn't be very pleasant going out with him in the evening if he remained as sullen as he looked at present.

'She suggested you came too. I can't go. I've got a parcel to collect. But let's finish the leaves first.'

'All right.' He began to sweep again.

'I'll go and see how the bonfire's getting on.'

Standing sniffing with half-shut eyes by the smoking pile of leaves Polly didn't realize she was observed until the kitchen window opened.

'Oh dear,' said the voice of Mrs. Mandeville, 'Garth was supposed to do that.'

'Yes, I'm helping.'

‘I should stand farther away, the smell will get into your clothes. Is it hurting your eyes? He’s naughty to let you.’

‘He couldn’t have stopped me. I like bonfires.’ She withdrew a couple of paces for the sake of politeness.

‘Oh well in that case . . .’ said Mrs. Mandeville, her voice trailing away uncertainly. She resumed: ‘Do you mind if I shut the window? Just so the smuts don’t fly in.’ She vanished behind the reflected sky in the glass, smile last like the Cheshire cat.

“How are we getting to your friend’s?’ asked Garth when the leaves were done.

‘Walking,’ said Polly briefly, wishing he would use Judith’s name. ‘None of the buses go from here to there.’ She didn’t add that it was a lovely day for a walk; he could see that.

‘I think I’ll bring my bicycle.’

‘Push it, do you mean?’

‘Yes. It’ll be convenient for coming back.’

‘We could both ride it there – not together,’ she added hastily, seeing his expression, ‘you could ride it a little way, then leave it and walk on, and when I got to it I could ride it until I caught you up, and so on.’

‘We’re not in a hurry, are we?’

‘Oh no. Perhaps it wouldn’t be any quicker anyway.’

‘It would be bound to be *quicker*. Somewhere between the walking time and the riding time.’

‘Anyway, if we’re going together I suppose we might as well go together.’

He said nothing to this and wheeled the gleaming Moulton for some time in silence, his eyes on the ground. Polly responded by taking an exaggerated interest in her surroundings. Brick and stone, flowers and trees, nothing could help looking good in the clear October sunshine.

'Supposing that the bike was always ridden for equal distances at the same constant speed,' said Garth presently, 'which implies that the distances walked would be equal to those ridden, and to each other, and supposing that the walking speeds were equal, then the time taken would be the average of the walking time and the riding time.'

'That's what you said before.'

'I didn't say it would be the average. It wouldn't, with the haphazard conditions you stated. The riding person would need to pass the walking person each time, and go on to the specified point. One could use lamp-posts.'

'Shall we try it out?'

'No.'

When they arrived Judith said Mark and Tom were playing table tennis in the garage.

'I've been cheering them on. Here's your parcel, Polly.'

'Goodness,' said Polly, staggering. 'It's heavy enough.'

'What exactly do you want it for? You never really said.'

Polly described her plans for the loft.

'So you never asked your father?' said Garth.

'Not yet. My mother seemed so sure he'd say no.'

'Yes,' said Judith dubiously. 'I hope you don't

intend to start doing things yourself with the help of this book?'

'Not without asking. I just want to search a bit into the possibilities.'

Mark and Tom finished their game and came to chat.

'Take you on when I've got my breath back?' said Tom to Judith.

'Perhaps Garth would like to play.'

'He and Mark can have next turn,' said Tom at once. His uneasiness with Garth reminded Polly of the wary way the boys at the technical college treated Kim.

'I don't actually want to play,' said Garth.

'Fine,' said Mark. 'I can talk to Polly. Good Lord, is that the thing Judith's been hiding for you?'

'Yes – be careful, it's only on approval. But I get this set of brushes to keep.'

'Handy,' said Mark, trying one out along the shelf.

'Was there a free gift with your machine, Garth?' she asked.

'No.' He sounded rather cold. Perhaps she shouldn't have mentioned it in front of the others. Weight reduction wasn't a problem to them; Tom was almost pathetic with his thin legs and hollow cheeks, and Mark was the kind of boy who gets called well made – not a description that could truthfully be applied to Garth.

'Coming to that war film at the Ritz tonight?' Mark asked Polly. 'We thought we'd all go.'

'I'm afraid I can't.' She felt regretful.

'Oh come on, be a devil. You haven't been out since the beginning of term.'

'I'm doing something with Garth,' she said quickly. She hadn't told anyone but Liz about *Lollipop Boy*; she suspected Judith would disapprove, and Mark would probably say what on earth did she want to see that for.

Her evasive statement put him off successfully. 'Well, I'm glad you're not working too hard,' he said after a moment. 'It doesn't suit you.'

'But as you said yourself you have got exams this year.' Garth couldn't let such a frivolous remark pass unchallenged.

'Polly doesn't care about exams any more than me.'

Wishing Garth didn't provoke people into these exaggerations, Polly said: 'I haven't had any important ones before. I should think I'm working harder than I did at school – that wouldn't be difficult of course.'

Judith and Tom finished their game just as Judith's mother called them all to tea. When they found it laid ready in the dining-room Polly guessed Mrs. Wilson must be between books. They saw very little of her when she was writing, and usually foraged for themselves in the kitchen. Dr. Wilson was there too.

'How's the tech?' he asked Polly.

'Still standing.' It was the kind of answer he liked.

'Could somebody pass the milk?' said Mrs. Wilson. 'Oh dear, no, that's the hot water. Have you burnt yourself?'

'It would be a service like any other. Your father said it worked.'

'He also said he wouldn't do it himself. They took people's money for nothing.'

'You can hardly call it nothing. Haven't you ever heard of psychosomatic cures?'

'Yes I have. They're done by quacks.'

They stared at each other without speaking for a moment. Mark was breathing hard, and Garth's colour was higher than usual.

'I think it would be a perfectly fair way to make money,' said Polly, who found the whole idea fascinating. 'People take a chance anyway when they pay for that kind of thing – charming and faith healing and all that. It's not like going to a doctor.'

'Oh, you might just as well set up a stall in the market and sell bottles of coloured water for rheumatism!' said Mark impatiently.

'Why not, if it cured the rheumatism?' said Garth.

'Why *not*?' expostulated Mark.

'I don't suppose it would cure rheumatism,' said Polly. 'Warts seem to be special. After all, if you could do everything that way you wouldn't need doctors any more.'

'Quite,' said Garth provocatively.

Tom and Judith exchanged glances.

'Wouldn't pay sixpence for it myself,' said Tom, 'or a penny, come to that. I'd sooner be sliced by your dad.'

'And he said you needn't be,' said Judith. 'Does anyone feel like another game of table tennis?'

'I must go,' said Garth.

Polly said she must as well, and parcelled up her book in its wrappings. She had found a section on lofts which she wanted to read at her leisure. One sentence gave her considerable trouble when she got home; she wished Garth was there to help. '*Area of ceiling at seven and a half feet from floor,*' she muttered to herself, '*must be greater than half area at five feet from floor. Area at seven and a half* ... oh, it's no good. I shall have to go up there and see.'

Downstairs she took the tape measure from the drawer of the sewing machine and noted that her mother was safely occupied in the kitchen, Michael and Jennifer were out and Hugh was reading a library book, flat on his stomach in front of the fire.

It was very difficult, she found, to measure anything while balancing on a joist in a poor light. And seven and a half feet was taller than either her or the tape measure. She could see that the ridge pole was higher still, and she could locate the point on the rafters where they were five feet from the floor – if floor it could be called, she thought grimly, as she wobbled in a dangerous fashion from one joist to the next – but that was about all. She sat down to calm her nerves and was thankful not to be standing a moment later when heavy footsteps came up the stairs. She had checked on the rest of the family, but had forgotten her father.

He said nothing when he reached the landing and she wondered if he could possibly not have noticed the ladder; only if that were the case why didn't he go away? He seemed to be standing, lost in thought perhaps, at the top of the stairs. Her leg was aching; she tried to shift it without making a noise.

'Take your time coming down, Polly.'

The quiet voice startled her far more than if he had been angry. Feeling very silly she crawled to the opening and descended.

'I hope you were careful of the plaster.'

'Yes,' she said meekly.

'Didn't your mother ask you not to go up there again?'

'I think that was the younger ones.' He took the ladder and put it away. 'I didn't know you knew about the other time.'

'Yes, we talked about it.'

'It wouldn't be terribly difficult to turn it into a room, would it?' she asked eagerly. 'It just wants floorboards and a window and a flight of stairs. You need to have planning permission, and a building inspector and a public health officer have to look at it, but if they say it's all right . . .'

'The rest is easy?' said her father drily. 'I must say you're very well informed.'

'I've got a book. It tells you everything. The only thing is I don't think they'll let you do it if the area at seven and a half feet isn't right. I was trying to measure. I'll get the book – I expect you'd understand that bit better than me.'

'Don't bother. A ceiling could be put in which would satisfy the requirements; I've already verified that.'

Polly was both snubbed and excited. 'You mean you're really considering it? Mummy didn't think you would.'

'I certainly shouldn't attempt the work myself – the window would need roof ladders and scaffolding, for a start. I know a man who might, though. We could insulate the roof at the same time; that should have been done long ago.' He changed to a warning tone. 'Of course, it'll need considerable discussion before we decide. You stay out of the loft in the meantime; and you'd better clean yourself up before your mother sees you.'

Some of the discussion took place downstairs as soon as Polly had followed his suggestion. Mrs. Devenish, unmoved by Polly's vision of a beautiful new room, thought they couldn't afford it and didn't fancy workmen in the house.

'It would cost less than a move, and cause less upheaval in the long run,' said her husband. 'And of course it increases the value of the property.'

They talked until Polly realized with a shock that she was going to be late meeting Garth if she didn't hurry. Getting ready, with the help of all she had borrowed from Liz, took longer than usual. She was quite awed by the result, and Hugh, meeting her on the stairs, exclaimed:

'*Crumbs.*'

'Be quiet,' said Polly, shaking her hair forward and turning up her coat collar. 'I'm just off,' she called to her mother as she opened the front door.

'Don't be late back. You're going with Mark and Judith, are you?'

'No, with Garth. Didn't I say?'

'No.' Her mother came into the hall as though inclined for further conversation.

'I can't stop,' said Polly, poised on the doorstep with averted head. 'I'll miss the bus.'

'Well,' said her mother again, 'don't be late back, will you.'

Polly sometimes went half on buses, but hadn't the nerve to try it that evening. Counting the money in her pocket she remembered the Gaumont was more expensive than the Ritz, and hoped Garth wouldn't object to the front stalls, which was where they usually sat when she went with the others. The bus was passing the Ritz now; the war film had started earlier and there was nobody outside. Looking at her reflection in the driver's shoulders she unfastened the top button of her coat and smoothed her hair. She didn't dare touch her face. Its equilibrium felt so delicate she was almost afraid to speak.

Garth, waiting outside the Gaumont, met her approach with an expression of total blankness.

'It's me,' she said, grinning nervously.

'Hallo,' he replied.

When he had suggested she could make herself look older he had had no picture in his head; he was quite unprepared for this transformation. Suddenly there seemed some point to his mother's anxious remarks when told of his plans for the evening. ('Outside the cinema? Couldn't you have gone to her house? It won't be very nice for her if she gets there first.' 'Oh, he never does anything properly,' his grandfather had said with disgust.)

'We'd better go in.' Annoyance helped Polly straighten her face. Garth was the one who'd suggested this disguise, and since he'd got to put up with it for the evening he might ask himself how she could be expected to carry it off if he looked at her in that horror-struck way.

'Yes,' said Garth. Even though she hadn't had to wait she seemed cross. He bought tickets for the circle in an effort at appeasement.

'Here, I can't afford that!'

'What do you mean?' he muttered. 'Were you going to pay for yourself?' He was embarrassed by the uniformed attendant who stood with impassive face, no doubt scorning his uncertainty.

'I do usually,' said Polly, uncertain in her turn.

He made up his mind. 'Well, when you're with me you don't.' It sounded all right; he stepped forward boldly, nodding in reply to the attendant's unnecessary gesture towards the stairs.

They settled into their seats and watched the advertisements come to an end. *Lollipop Boy*, the screen informed them, had been passed fit for showing when no member of the audience was under eighteen.

Before it was half-way through Garth was wishing he'd taken Polly to the despised war film. At least they might perhaps have held hands in the thrilling parts. There was nothing to hold hands about here. Bored and baffled, he gazed at a close-up of a foot which had just trodden on a thorn. A bead of blood oozed from the calloused heel and was licked away; not, he thought, by the owner of the foot.

He bought ice creams in the interval. 'What do you think of it?' he asked her.

'What do you?'

'I asked first.'

Polly licked her ice. 'They're all such nasty people.'

'Yes.'

When the lights dimmed he asked suddenly: 'You do want to stay for the rest?'

'Oh, we must. It might get better.'

Events did move with a little more speed, simply because the characters grew nastier. The title part was the most repulsive young boy Polly had ever seen; she felt the actor was probably repulsive in real life as well.

Like the Ritz, the Gaumont had dispensed with the national anthem long ago. As Polly stumbled out on cramped limbs she heard someone whistling it to make up, and glanced over the packed heads. It was Kim. He was with Louise.

'Someone you knew?' asked Garth as they reached fresh air. Kim had smiled and waved; Louise had simply smiled. Polly hoped she'd managed to respond.

'He's at the tech. They both are.'

'Oh.' His tone seemed to suggest that nothing about the tech need be taken seriously. It was as though it didn't exist. Presumably it didn't for him.

'Which way is your bus stop?' asked Polly.

'I'll come home with you first.'

'It's a bit late.'

'That's why.'

'Oh I see. I don't think I need anyone really. But come if you want to.'

He came. They had used all possible remarks by the time they got off the bus, and along Polly's road they walked in silence. Once the backs of their hands brushed together; Polly removed hers as automatically as if it had knocked against a wall. She was thinking about Kim and Louise.

They said good-bye at her gate. Wondering if she ought to thank him for the film, Polly decided she'd already done it when he bought the tickets. After he'd gone she remembered she hadn't; but she could hardly shout it down the street. At any rate she was pretty sure she'd said thank you for the ice.

Although she tried to unlock the front door quietly the hall light clicked on before she was inside.

'There you are,' said her mother; then in a different voice: 'Good heavens, what do you look like!'

Polly stood blinking helplessly.

'Worse than Hugh said!'

'I expect it's a bit messed up by now.'

'It can't have been any better when it wasn't. How did you manage to buy so much stuff?'

'Most of it's borrowed from Liz.'

'Well, that was kind of her I suppose.' She sounded unconvinced. 'Do you really need to go to all this trouble for Garth?'

'Not for *Garth*. I wanted to look older.'

'Oh you do make me cross.' Mrs. Devenish closed the front door with a sharp snap. 'One day you'll be sorry you wished your youth away.'

'The film was an X,' said Polly, bored with the whole conversation.

'An X? *What* X?'

Anyone would think X films were the end.

'*Lollipop Boy*,' said Polly, her voice faltering

slightly as it occurred to her that perhaps this one was. 'I think I'll go and wash,' she added.

'Yes, you'd better. And get ready for bed, it's late enough.'

As Polly went she heard her mother repeating incredulously '*Lollipop Boy!*'

For once Jennifer was asleep. Polly put on her pyjamas but stopped short of brushing her teeth; her stomach felt terribly empty. She went to the bottom of the stairs and stood for a few moments listening to her mother's feet as she marched from kitchen to living-room and back again. Perhaps she wasn't hungry after all. She turned to go back upstairs.

'Do you want a cup of tea?' called her mother sharply.

'Yes please,' said Polly, turning again on the step that creaked.

Mrs. Devenish was tidying. She always worked hardest when she was angry.

'Did you enjoy it?' she asked, piling some of Polly's belongings into her arms as she passed.

'It was peculiar.'

'Don't ask me to explain anything, because I probably shouldn't be able to.'

'All right.'

'And don't say all right like that!' She banged two used mugs down on the drainer so hard that one of them broke. Polly looked fearfully at the pieces, and then at her mother, who laughed. She picked up the larger fragments while Polly went for a dust-pan.

'We just wondered what it would be like,' said

Polly as they sat over their cup of tea a few minutes later.

'And what was it like?'

'Not worth seeing.'

'Then I shan't bother.'

'Why don't you and Daddy go sometimes? Wouldn't you like to?'

'We do go sometimes. What about Jennifer's birthday treat?'

'But that was her ninth birthday, nearly two years ago!'

'We went a good deal when we were younger.' She gazed absently at her spoon.

'Oh dear,' said Polly, 'it seems so sad.'

'Good heavens, I don't mind! Drink up that tea and get along to bed. You sound a bit overtired to me.'

Polly went, although she knew she would lie awake for some time. She thought first about the film, then about Kim, then about her room in the roof. If they kept the skylight as well as a new window she would have her bed-head underneath it and look up to stars. She could have a cord hanging by her pillow to pull the curtain. A curtain for a sloping window would need a rod top and bottom; it would be like a sliding door. Matching curtains for the bigger window, and cushions perhaps on a window seat . . . there wouldn't be much furniture to take from here, only her bed really (and she could fight Jennifer for the chest of drawers) so the more they could build in the better. Cupboards, with shelves above; she could keep all her books there; and a sizeable mirror on the wall. It would be well worth seeing when it was finished. She could take people on conducted tours, or perhaps have a room-warming party.

She had been sliding towards sleep, but the notion of a party woke her up. She hadn't had one of her own for years. She was old enough now for it to be entirely her own; very lively, she thought, with dancing, and wine. She could ask Kim.

The first objection would be money. Her mother might fairly say that if she was giving it she should pay. She hadn't noticed any Saturday jobs going recently, and she couldn't work on the post until Christmas. Perhaps she could charm a few warts.

Yes, wart charming; why not? The more she thought about this idea the better it seemed. No good hoping her parents would allow her to do it at home, though; and she couldn't believe Judith would let her use her address for such a scheme, or indeed want anything to do with it. Judith tended to be conventional.

It occurred to her that if she advertised her services in the personal column of the local paper it could all be managed by post without her confronting any warty people herself. According to Garth she'd be helping them just as much if she didn't; they only needed to believe in her. And presumably they wouldn't waste their money without at least an element of belief. She could use a box number and remain completely anonymous.

She spent some time drafting advertisements in her head and finally got it down to ten words:

Wart charming by post. Sixpence a wart. Send postal order. She couldn't be bothered to get out of bed, but she said it over several times to aid her memory before going to sleep. She would go during tomorrow's lunch hour and see about getting it put into the paper.

Mark sighed.

'Do cheer up,' said his mother. 'If you're going to spend the entire evening drooping it would have been better to see the film in the first place.'

'That was a yawn,' said Mark hastily.

'Perhaps you should go to bed.'

'I expect I will in a little while.'

'There's not much point waiting up for them. Even if Polly does come in she won't be able to stay long.'

'Polly?' he said blankly, and after a moment: 'What do you mean, Polly?

His mother shrugged. 'Oh yes Mark, all right, I get your point. Nothing is farther from your thoughts at this moment than Polly.'

'Well, but Judith didn't go with Polly. She went with Tom.'

It was his mother's turn to look blank. 'Tom? Are you sure? She said she was going with Polly.'

'No she didn't, Ma. She couldn't have.'

'She said it would be just the two of them,' Mrs. Wilson remembered slowly.

'Yes, her and Tom.'

'I didn't realize that was what she meant.' She turned in her chair to face him more directly. 'Why on earth should she go without Polly or you?'

'Well,' said Mark, at a loss. Even if he could find the right words, the answer was too obvious to give.

'It seems so peculiar!'

'But Ma,' he said impatiently, 'you know about Judith and Tom.'

After a moment she said: 'I thought Tom was your friend.'

'Well, he is. And hers as well.' Now that he came to think of it, they had started to grow fond of each other while his mother was writing her last book; but he hadn't realized she was so completely unaware of the situation. Nor, he was sure, had Judith.

'What time is it?' she asked, looking at her watch.

Mark was pretending to concentrate on the television. He glanced indifferently at the clock and said: 'They won't be back yet.'

'But she's so young,' said his mother involuntarily.

'She's the same age as Polly.'

'Yes; really not very old.'

'You mean you'd be sitting here like a cat on hot bricks if I'd gone alone with Polly?'

'Of course not, Mark, don't be silly.'

'Well then.'

'It would be quite different.'

'I can't see why. You've known Tom ages.'

'Yes.'

'What have you got against him?' Mark was becoming indignant. 'You've never criticized him before.'

'One doesn't if one can help it,' said his mother absently, looking again at her watch.

'He's a very nice chap. If he can see anything in Judith you ought to be pleased.'

'You're being ridiculous, Mark. I wish you'd go to bed.'

'I'm trying to watch this programme,' he complained.

'Well for goodness' sake watch it then,' said his mother, quite as though she hadn't started the conversation in the first place.

They were silent for a while. Mark would have gone to bed if he hadn't been told to. He was just thinking that Tom and Judith ought really to be back by now when he heard them at the door.

'Hallo,' said Judith, 'goodness, it's warm in here. I've persuaded Tom to come in for some coffee; he thought it was too late.' She was holding him by the hand. The cold had coloured her cheeks and made her eyes shine; she looked quite pretty, thought Mark in surprise.

'It is a bit late,' agreed Mrs. Wilson.

'We just missed a bus,' mumbled Tom, detaching himself quickly under her eye.

'We didn't feel like waiting half an hour for the next so we walked. We tried to get here before it caught us up; we nearly managed it.' Judith unfastened her coat. She was wearing the dress she had made a few weeks before. Mrs. Wilson looked from Tom's tie to the dress and back to the tie. They matched.

'Was the film any good?' asked Mark, seeing Tom's embarrassment.

'It was very gripping while we were watching it,' said Judith, 'but I don't think I want to go again.'

'Hey, guess who we saw coming out of *Lollipop Boy*,' exclaimed Tom.

'Who?'

'Polly. And that Garth chap.'

'Good heavens, how very unsuitable!' said Mrs. Wilson. He felt a twinge of guilt, but at least he had diverted her attention from his tie.

'So that's why she wouldn't come with us,' said Mark.

'I suppose she thought *Lollipop Boy*'d be a bit more exciting.'

'Exciting is hardly the word I'd have chosen,' said Mrs. Wilson crisply.

'No.' Tom wouldn't have chosen it either; he had only meant that Polly might. 'Well,' he said. 'I think I'd better be getting along.'

'Don't do that,' protested Judith. 'I'll make the coffee at once; you just sit down and talk to Mark for a few minutes.'

Tom thought of sitting talking to Mark under Mrs. Wilson's disapproving eye. She had always made him feel rather nervous. 'It's a bit late,' he said, unconsciously repeating her very words.

'Might your mother be worrying?' asked Mrs. Wilson.

Tom mumbled something, unsure what the right answer should be.

'We mustn't keep you in that case.'

Judith, disappointed, saw him out. Mark joined her in the kitchen while she made her own coffee.

'I wonder what Polly wanted to see that kinky film for,' he said.

'Mm.'

'She might have told us where she was going.'

'Mm.'

'I wonder why she didn't?'

'I should have warned Tom not to mention it,' said Judith impatiently.

'Why? Did Polly say I wasn't to know?'

'She didn't even realize we saw her. But I should have guessed you'd go on and on.'

'You are snappy. I suppose it's because Ma wouldn't let Tom stay.'

'I don't see why she wouldn't, do you?'

'Yes. She thinks you're too young to go out with him by yourself.' He rather enjoyed her stunned face.

After a pause she said: 'How silly.'

6

Just as Polly came down to breakfast the postman put the letters through the door. She was able to look at them first, as she had tried to do every morning recently. One for her father, one for her mother, two for her! They had both been forwarded by the local paper; they must be people answering her advertisement. She hadn't really believed anyone would.

The most ticklish part of getting the advertisement into the *Stilwell Herald* had been when she discovered that, box number or not, her name and address had to go at the bottom of the form. Suppose somebody who knew her father noticed the Devenish? But it would have looked rather odd to walk out of the office at that stage? and she had never heard that her father did know anyone who worked on the paper. She had gone ahead, and certainly the girl behind the counter had scanned the form with a totally expressionless face, counting the words with her biro as though they received wart-charming advertisements every day of the week.

Leaving the other letters where they lay Polly took hers to the living-room and shut them quickly and furtively into her case.

'Any cornflakes?' she asked her mother.

'No, I'm afraid we're down to the shreddybrek.'

'I don't know why you buy those things,' she complained, cutting herself a slice of bread. 'They're like haystacks.'

'*Straw* stacks,' said Hugh.

'Your father likes them because they don't go soggy.'

'They couldn't. They're man-made fibre.' She buttered her bread and coated it thickly with brown sugar.

'You're rather dressed up today,' said her mother.

Polly was wearing a brightly patterned blouse with a long dark velvet skirt she had made from curtains bought at the church jumble sale.

'Oh, everyone at tech wears these,' she replied airily. 'They're warmer.'

'You look like one of those sausages that go at the bottom of the doors,' observed Hugh.

Polly ignored him. She had promised Liz to go dancing after lunch today. Her hair, washed the evening before, had spent the night in a net and was now curving satisfactorily round her face. Before leaving she dashed into her parents' room and borrowed her mother's bottle of scent.

'I'm sure she won't notice, she's had it for years,' she told Jonathan. He frowned at her and uttered a series of short sharp cries like a motorbike revving up.

It was algebra first. She walked faster than usual because it wouldn't do to be late for Dr. Makepiece, and arrived a few minutes before nine. There was time to open her mail.

'Dear Sir,' said the first letter, 'Re your ad in the *Stilwell Herald* the fourteenth of inst and see you do warts charming. I have, in all sixteen warts on both my hands which at sixpence a wart I make, eight shillings. Please find inclosed postal order for which amount and oblidge, yours truly, A. B. Potts.'

The second envelope contained nothing but a postal order for five shillings signed R. Alsop. They gave Polly an uneasy thrill. She tucked them away at the bottom of her case and hoped Garth's theory of psychosomatic cures was sound.

Dad was idly covering the board with an intricate diagram in which miles of tubing led from tanks to jars to narrow-necked flasks. 'Very good,' said Sandy, and wrote at the bottom *Please leave* followed by a squiggle. Footsteps sounded in the corridor and Dad grabbed the duster, but too late; Dr. Makepiece was turning the doorhandle. Dad fled like Sandy to a seat.

'Good morning,' said the Doctor, and looked hard at the board. 'Can anyone read those initials?'

Nobody replied. He turned and strode out, returning in a few minutes with a folding blackboard which he proceeded to erect, watched by Dad with dropped jaw.

'Now!' he said finally, facing the class and knocking his hands together. 'Any homework diff—'

'It was me, sir,' said Dad.

'Oh it *was* was it, Alsop. Right. You can just take this back to room 21 where it came from, and explain to Mr. Routledge why you're interrupting his lecture for the second time.'

'Yes sir,' said Dad gloomily, leaving his seat and seizing one end of the board.

'You'd better disassemble it first.'

'Oh. Yes sir.'

'I'll help him, sir,' offered Sandy.

'Will you? Why?'

'I wrote the bit at the bottom, sir.'

Dr. Makepiece gazed at him for half a minute before saying: 'Fair enough. Get on with it.'

'Did you explain to Mr. Routledge?' he asked when they returned.

'We said we didn't need it after all, sir.'

'Sanders, you'd make a good politician.'

They went on with the lecture.

'Er – Miss Cartwright,' he said at the end, 'I'd like to see you in my office at one today.'

'Ooh,' breathed Liz, rounding her eyes at Polly. 'Righto sir.'

'I suppose that means we can't go dancing,' said Polly when he had gone.

'Have a heart! However long do you think he wants me for?'

Polly, who had already begun feeling disappointed (or relieved, she wasn't sure which) rearranged her ideas.

'Won't take more than ten minutes, I bet you.'

In fact it was five past one when she returned to the classroom where Polly was cleaning her shoes with a tissue and putting scent behind her ears.

'Do you know what he told me to do?' she burst out.

'No, what?' said Polly, all agog.

'Lengthen my skirt!'

Polly, secure in her velvet, laughed. 'It is rather short,' she said.

'I'm wearing matching pants. I don't know what more I can be expected to do.'

'Did you tell him that?'

'I was going to show him – I dropped my bag on the way out, but you know his starchy manners; he was round the desk to pick it up before I could bend over.'

'Perhaps you could let in a strip of material in a gay contrasting colour,' suggested Polly.

Liz giggled. 'No, but it's my favourite dress. I'm wearing it specially for Mr. Norris.'

'What will you drop in front of him?'

'Polly!' Liz made a point of being shocked by her whenever possible; she once explained 'It's so unexpected somehow when you say things like that.'

They went down to the hall. It wasn't one of Jim Bicks' days; the music was provided by a giant radiogram, the pride of the student union. Against the wall were piles of stacking chairs, and a row of tables pushed end to end on which sat and leaned a number of boys. Liz was claimed almost at once by a yellow-haired giant in studded torturer's boots. Polly, watching the couples, noticed Kim with a girl she had never seen before. Her heart gave a thump, and she thanked God she wasn't prone to blushes. She didn't give him a chance to catch her eye.

One of the latest hits came to an end and was replaced by another. The couples broke apart and reformed, some who had been more energetic falling out for a rest.

'Dance?' said a pair of black corduroy jeans, appearing in front of Polly.

'Oh! Yes, all right.'

He was black corduroy all the way up to his pink shirt collar and black corduroy hair. Polly followed him into the middle of the room where he stopped abruptly, faced her and began to dance. She tried to move and found she couldn't; her limbs had forgotten everything they'd learned. Having started by holding Liz's hands she had found it quite easy to graduate to managing without; with this stranger she was unexpectedly helpless. He kept his hands strictly to himself and his eyes fixed on a point behind her left shoulder. It didn't seem to matter to him whether she joined in or not. Polly decided for herself that it was either dance or leave the floor; picking a girl a few yards distant she started to copy her movements, and felt her panic subside.

'Seen you in here before, haven't I,' said black corduroy.

'No, I don't think so. I mean no, you couldn't have.'

'Secretarial, are you?'

'Not actually.'

'Nurse?'

'I'm doing ordinary levels.'

'Oh,' he said with infinite boredom.

'What about you?'

'I know all about levels, I do.'

'Do you? Why?'

'Railway engineer.'

Polly smiled politely. His face remained blank, leading her to wonder whether hers had in fact obeyed the signal sent by her brain, or even whether he might suffer from a similar disability.

'Going to be,' he said.

'Going to be what?'

'A railway engineer.'

'Oh I see. Sorry.'

'Wasn't my toe.'

Polly felt she couldn't attempt to sort this out. She was glad when the music ended. Black corduroy left her without a word and barged purposefully towards another girl, while Polly went and leaned on the tables with feigned exhaustion. Kim was walking in her direction; no; he had turned aside and found Louise. As the dancing started again she noticed in a far corner Sandy, Dad and Boris. They had arranged some chairs and tables so that they could do their homework while looking on. She might have gone along for a chat if she hadn't suddenly felt, as her mother had suggested, rather dressed up. Ridiculously so, even. Liz was happily occupied with a new partner; she probably wouldn't mind if Polly didn't stay. She decided to wait for the end of the present song, which happened to be one of her favourites, and then leave.

On her way to the door she was stopped by Kim.

'You're not going, are you?'

'I was,' said Polly.

'But do dance with me first.'

Kim was of the energetic class; without touching Polly he managed to communicate his wishes, and she found him a far easier partner than black corduroy. She began to enjoy herself.

'What did you think of *Lollipop Boy*?' he asked.

Polly was thrown out of step, remembering Louise. 'Not much,' she said.

'Oh really? Why not?'

'I didn't like any of the people.'

'No goodies, true. But plenty of baddies.'

'You can't have one without the other, can you?'

'I suppose you can't,' he conceded with respect. 'And they weren't, really. They were trapped by their personalities – except the boy.'

'He was the worst of the lot.'

'Well, he was trapped by them.'

'I don't see that at all. He didn't have to be what they expected him to be.'

'It's not so easy. Everyone's trapped one way or another; that's the human condition.'

'I'm not,' said Polly roundly, 'and I don't believe you are either.'

'You'd be surprised.' Kim grinned. 'Think of one's parents, for a start.'

'Did yours mind you seeing the film?'

'I didn't tell them. Anything for peace.'

'I told my mother in a fit of temper.'

Kim laughed. He had a most endearing laugh. 'What happened?'

'She carried on a bit and broke a mug, and then it was all right.'

'That doesn't sound too bad,' he said, laughing still.

'And what about Louise's?' She hadn't intended to ask any such thing.

'I don't know Louise's parents.'

Miserable, Polly danced a little harder. He meant she should mind her own business and leave

Louise out of the conversation. Or perhaps it was a way of saying that Louise didn't matter? Of course he didn't know Polly's parents, wasn't within miles of meeting them; but if he came to her room-warming party . . .

'You're good at this,' said Kim.

'Am I really?'

'Yes; particularly in those clothes.'

'I made the skirt out of curtains.' Listening to herself Polly wondered seriously if the company of another person could cause one to be drunk.

'Just like Scarlett O'Hara,' said Kim.

'Have *you* read that?'

'Yes, but don't tell anyone. It was in the house. I had chicken pox and I was driving them mad, and my mother chained it to the bed and promised me half a crown if I didn't want to go on after the first chapter.' He looked doleful. 'I succumbed.'

'I read it three times,' admitted Polly.

'That's far worse than me. Did you fall in love with Ashley?'

'No, he was a twerp. I liked Rhett. I don't fall in love with book people much.'

'Do you at all?'

'Well, Renny Whiteoak . . .' Kim looked blank. 'In the Jalna books. But not any more,' said Polly hastily.

'Natasha in *War and Peace*,' supplied Kim.

'I haven't read it yet.'

'Oh, you must.'

She knew she would; if she hadn't intended to before, she did now. 'Is that in the house as well?'

'I don't believe so,' said Kim vaguely. The music was ending; he took Polly's hand and bowed. 'Thank you,' he said.

'I enjoyed it,' said Polly, and didn't notice that the silence from the gramophone was continuing until Liz appeared, asking:

'Fun?'

'Yes.'

'You'll come again, won't you?'

'I might, I suppose.'

'I love your skirt,' said Louise, passing by. 'Did you know your blouse is coming astray at the back?'

Tucking it in Polly watched her catch up with Kim in the doorway and saw his smile.

They had Mr. Norris, and then there was a physics practical for Polly.

'I'm going to be right bright today,' said Dad as they waited to be let into the lab.

'Oh yes?' said Sandy.

'Yes. I'm tired of him saying I don't do things properly. Hey, did I tell you I'm getting my warts seen to?'

'Are you? How?'

'There was this ad in the paper. Charming by post. I had to send five shillings.'

'That should make you very charming,' said Sandy.

Polly's bottled feelings escaped in a smile. Somehow it had never occurred to her that the R. Alsop of the postal order might be him.

Boris glanced at Dad's hands and pronounced: 'They took your money for nowt.' Polly, considering his round dark head and saturnine face, wondered if his mother really was a Russian dancer. Impossible to ask.

The afternoon's experiment involved bunsen burners and boiling water, and small weights which had to be tied up and dangled inside a metal vessel in the steam. Polly spent some time trying to find a good place to attach the other end of her string before she noticed the boys were simply wedging theirs with the cork that closed the top of the vessel. She lit her bunsen burner and went to sign for a thermometer in the lab notebook. Boris had written his name in the wrong column. 'Where's B. Jones? I want to borrow B. Jones!' said one of the boys.

Dad was busy at the balance, frowning over one of the smallest weights. Polly didn't use the tiny ones; she reckoned the general standard of her work didn't call for such accuracy. 'Can you read what it says?' he asked Sandy.

'That's not a weight, it's a bit of silver paper.'

Polly dreamily recorded temperatures and thought about Kim. Suppose she invited him to her party and he didn't come? She hadn't told anyone at home about her plans yet; her father had said the day before that the work on the loft was a certainty, and she thought this was enough for her mother to be going on with.

'These thermometers are no good,' said Sandy. 'They bend when you put them in water.'

Mr. Leigh went out for a moment, and some of the boys took advantage of his absence to join two taps with a piece of rubber tubing and turn them both full on. 'It was an experiment to determine the strength of the rubber, sir,' they said when he returned to find everything drenched in the neighbourhood of the sink. Even the ceiling was wet.

'It's dripped into my calorimeter,' complained Dad.

'Put that when you write it up,' advised Sandy. 'This result is inaccurate due to drips which fell from the ceiling. Go on, you ought to; we're supposed to put everything.'

'I knelt on the floor to look at the image of the pin . . .' said Polly. 'Sir came along and fell over my legs. He said certain words. Anyone wishing to see these words please look at the end of my book.'

Sandy liked this so much Mr. Leigh had to ask for less noise.

Polly took out her cork to see how the steam was getting on. The weight promptly dropped right inside, its string vanishing faster than she could grab. Luckily there was another way in at the base. Some of the steam would probably have condensed by now; pleased with herself for remembering this she started to unscrew. Out came a little water, and out too came the weight, straight through the bottom of the beaker she had so prudently placed beneath.

'I did say less noise in this corner,' remarked Mr. Leigh, coming to investigate. Polly, incapable of speech, pointed at the calamity. One of the boys was sent for a dustpan, which she couldn't help thinking carried preferential treatment a little far; she quickly recovered enough to pick up the pieces herself.

'I'm awfully sorry, sir,' she said.

'Never mind, Miss Devenish,' he replied wearily.

'It's a little late to start again; you'd better just write up the experiment as far as you'd got.'

'Yes sir,' said Polly, trying not to look at Sandy in case he made her laugh again. Even when going home she couldn't think of it without being obliged to take out her handkerchief and pretend to blow her nose.

'Remember you've got that great book to pack up,' said her mother after tea.

'Mm.'

'You'd better do it next; you'll only forget otherwise.'

'Mm.'

'You'll find yourself having to pay for it if it doesn't go back tomorrow. Polly, are you listening to me?'

She looked up from her diary. 'Yes, of course.'

'Do you think you ought to spend so much time on that story or whatever it is? You haven't even started your homework yet, have you?'

'Mr. Routledge thinks it's a good idea for me to do some writing.'

'Are you sure he meant in your examination year?'

'Any time,' said Polly firmly.

'When will you read it to us?' asked Hugh.

'I shall NOT read it to you.'

'Never mind, when it's a book we can buy it,' said Michael.

'Good lord, it won't be published,' exclaimed Polly with such horror that he blushed. She put it away; it was impossible to think of the right words with everyone badgering.

'I can't find it,' she said a few minutes later.

'What?' asked her mother.

'The Do-it-yourself.'

'Oh Polly, I hope to goodness you haven't lost it. I don't know why you wanted to send for it in the first place; you might have known Daddy wouldn't be very impressed.'

'Well, I did get those free brushes.'

'They won't be free when you've paid the return postage, will they? Go and look in the front room; if it's not there I suppose we'll all have to start searching.'

'Ruddy hellfire,' muttered Hugh.

'It's all right,' said Polly, coming back. 'Daddy was reading it.'

Mrs. Devenish sighed with exasperation. 'He would choose now.'

'He says he'll pack it later himself.' She sat down and took out her homework books. 'When I get my loft room I'll work up there,' she remarked.

'If you get it,' said her mother.

'Daddy's asked the man to come!'

'Oh yes I know. But I can't really believe in anything except the mess at this stage.'

'I can,' said Polly.

7

It was Saturday morning. On her way to buy more paint, Polly met Mark.

'Hallo! How are you?' he said.

'Fine.'

'Judith's been missing you.'

'You mean since she came round on Thursday evening?'

'Well no, I suppose I meant before that really.'

'I've been so busy,' said Polly vaguely, 'with my room and things.'

'She told me about your room.'

'Yes.' Polly became animated. 'Just wait until you see it. I'm having a room-warming party when it's all done.'

'I thought it was all done?'

'Oh no. The builder's gone, but it needs an awful lot of finishing.'

'Good morning, Polly,' said the brisk voice of an elderly man approaching at a smart walk.

'Oh hallo Mr. Mandeville.' Polly leaped to one side to allow him room to pass.

'Beautiful day,' he remarked.

'A bit cold,' said Polly.

'Not if you keep moving. Haven't I met you before, young man?'

'Er – yes sir,' said Mark. People sirred Garth's

grandfather automatically; Polly had a job not to do it herself. She thought it might be connected with his having been a senior master at Garth's school.

'Mark Wilson,' said Mr. Mandeville, nodding sharply.

'That's right, sir.'

'I thought I remembered you. Good morning.'

'Good morning, sir.'

He left them. Mark shrugged and said: 'Where was I? Oh yes, how about the cinema this evening? There's a good film on.'

Polly considered for a moment. 'No, I don't think I will.'

'You used to come quite often,' said Mark, eyes on the ground.

'Well, I told you I've been busy.'

'Have you stopped going out altogether?'

'Of course not,' said Polly, without bothering to think whether this was in fact true.

'Everyone needs a break sometimes.'

'Actually I can't afford it at the moment.'

'You afforded it with Garth.' Mark suddenly looked her in the face.

'He paid.'

There was a short silence.

'Well, good-bye,' began Polly, feeling rather ashamed of herself.

'I'll pay, of course, if you want to come tonight,' said Mark stiffly.

'Oh heavens, I've already said I don't!' It would be impossible to tell him that the only person she wanted to go out with was Kim, and unreasonable to expect him to guess; but need he go on and on?

She almost longed for the days when he had been a simple foe.

'Oh,' said Mark with abrupt enlightenment. 'I suppose you can't.'

'No. I can't.' Let him make what he liked of that.

She bought her paint and started home. She was finding her free gift very useful, though her father sniffed and said she would never get anywhere with those silly little things. Neither would he lend her a better one; 'I'm not having her using my good brushes,' was what he said.

Polly was quite content to use her own. She thought she was managing very nicely. Her father sometimes strolled up after she'd gone to bed and put on a second coat.

The worst of the mess was over now. The builder had gone, taking his assistant, a blue-eyed whistling boy who reminded Polly of Sandy, in his reluctance to communicate as much as anything else. By the time they departed he would just about wink at her when he met her, though he talked back quite sharply to Hugh. They left behind a long light room, with a fragrance of new wood which Polly wished would stay for ever, even while she busily overlaid it with the smell of paint. The stairs were built of wood with overlapping treads; 'a sort of glorified ladder?' Polly's mother said, but 'No, a ladder would be illegal,' said Mr. Devenish, and Polly put in indignantly 'This is what modern stairs are *like*.'

Having used a fair quantity of the fresh paint Polly sat down for a rest. She had got the seat she'd wanted, under the new dormer window; it was part of the cupboards along that wall. She also had her little star-watching window, which had caused great envy among the younger ones, even Michael sounding quite wistful as he explained to Hugh (who already knew perfectly well) how such a thing wouldn't be possible in their own room.

Up here the telephone wasn't audible, but she heard Jennifer's shout from the landing. 'Polly! One of your boy friends ringing up!'

'Who?' She wasn't going to rush down full of hope for nothing. Jennifer could usually put a name to a voice if asked, only she preferred to make it sound as though Polly knew legions of boys.

'Garth!'

'Oh.' She descended the stairs and picked up the receiver. 'Hallo.'

'I thought you might have come round today.' He sounded woebegone.

'Why, had your mother made a cake?' She continued hastily before he had time to be insulted, 'I couldn't have said I was, surely? I haven't seen you.'

'No. Quite.'

'Well, I've been rather busy with my new room.'

'Isn't it finished yet?'

'Heavens no, there's tons to do.'

'Oh. Well anyway, will you come out with me tonight?'

He didn't seem to expect or even want an affirmative reply. 'Out where?' she stalled.

'I don't know. We could see a film if you liked.'

'I can't actually,' she said, trying not to be too irritated by his lackadaisical manner. 'Perhaps another time.'

'Grandfather saw you with Mark today.'

'Did he,' said Polly, bored.

'He said he spoke to you.'

'Yes.' She decided to ring off in a moment.

('An athletic-looking youngster,' Mr. Mandeville had said, running a disparaging eye over his grandson.

'The only thing he thinks about is games,' Garth had sulkily replied.

'Not everyone possesses academic ability. Has Polly been out with you lately?'

'I haven't asked her.'

'I see.' He had gone on to talk about defeatist attitudes and the need for exercise until Garth excused himself on the pretext of cleaning his bike.)

'He'd like it if you came round,' he said now.

Bordigals, thought Polly, he'd do better enticing me with cake. 'That wouldn't be going out, would it?' she replied.

'You won't, then?'

'I don't think so.'

'Would you if I was someone else?'

She was shaken. 'Yes. I would.' Uncaring, she allowed the truth to sound in her voice.

'Good-bye,' he said after a moment, and replaced the receiver with the gentlest of clicks.

'Polly can't come this evening,' said Mark to Judith.

'Oh. Why not?'

'How should I know?'

'Never mind,' said Judith with deliberate calm. 'How about you?'

'I shan't bother. It sounds a silly film anyway; no wonder she doesn't want to see it.'

'I suppose that means you and Tom will be going alone,' said Mrs. Wilson.

'Yes.'

'Well, please see you're not late back.'

Judith promised, wondering why her mother was making such a point of it. She put on new boots and a belted coat of soft wool, and tucked a wispy scarf round her neck.

'Have a good time,' said Mark gloomily.

After she had gone he watched television for a while and then went to bed. He had a premonition that his mother might start nagging if he didn't.

'Is it just us again?' said Tom when they met.

'Yes, Polly couldn't come.'

'Poor old Mark.' He looked at her sideways, not sure how far he was allowed to criticize her friend.

'She has been rather inaccessible since she went to the tech,' she agreed.

'Well, she hasn't got a boy friend there,' said Tom bluntly. 'Not that I've noticed. I think it's that chap Garth.'

'Perhaps it is. I don't seem to know her so well any more.'

'She doesn't still mind about you and me, does she?'

'No, I'm sure not. She hasn't for ages.'

The film was weak but enjoyable. They laughed

at the same things all the way through; quietly, out of regard for the audience, who didn't always share their view of what was funny.

'I've got a pain,' said Judith afterwards. 'It's hard to laugh in a whisper.'

'Bad?'

'No, it just needs a cup of coffee.'

'Let's go and have one at the Mocha.'

It wouldn't take long to get home (there was a bus due) but Judith remembered her mother hadn't been very welcoming last time she'd brought Tom in after the cinema. 'Yes, let's,' she said, shivering enjoyably at the prospect of warmth.

The Mocha was steamed up and noisy. Tom chose the table farthest from the juke box and brought over two coffees.

'You don't eat your froth off first,' he said.

'No, that's cheating. I try to make it last the whole drink through.'

They sipped, and let the music circle their ears without finding much of a way in. Tom finished the sugar at the bottom of both cups.

'Brown never stirs in properly.'

'You know you can buy special coffee sugar that tastes of coffee?'

'I expect they get it from the bottoms of cups.'

'We ought to hurry,' said Judith, drowsily reluctant, 'or I'll miss the last bus.'

She missed the last bus.

'Oh well, walk again I suppose.' She thought of her promise to be back early, and remembered with some disquiet that her mother had seemed to consider them late the time before. Sensing her uneasiness Tom said: 'We could do scouts' pace – walk for twenty and run for twenty.'

'Miles?'

'Paces!'

They tried it. 'Of course,' said Tom, 'scouts wouldn't be holding hands.'

He had been asked if he were a boy scout two days earlier, when he showed what Mr. Routledge considered a startling lack of common sense. 'I was once, sir,' he'd said.

'You'd never think it!'

'Oh, I'm not now sir. The scoutmaster disbanded the troop.'

'No idea of self-defence,' Polly had said, recounting this story to Judith.

'None at all,' Judith had agreed, her dimple appearing.

As they approached the Wilsons' house they walked slower and slower.

'Good-night then,' said Tom, stopping just short of the gate.

'Good-night,' said Judith, moving close. Nobody could see.

Mrs. Wilson opened the front door before Judith could put her key in the lock.

'Where's Tom?' she asked.

'He thought it was too late to come in.'

'Yes, I imagine he would.' Her tone seemed to accuse him of a number of things, rudeness and cowardice among them. Judith stepped inside quickly and closed the door.

'We missed the last bus,' she said, taking off her coat.

'The *last* bus? How?'

'We were too slow, I suppose.'

'You must have been extremely slow, considering the film ended over an hour ago. Or so they told me when I rang the cinema.'

'Rang the cinema?' repeated Judith, her voice colourless with astonishment.

'Yes, of course. Do you expect us just to sit twiddling our thumbs when you're over an hour late home?'

'I couldn't have come instantaneously,' Judith said half to herself.

Her father appeared on slow feet and she greeted him with relief. It had been one of his evenings in; he was wearing slippers.

'Hallo Judith.' He turned to his wife. 'Was there some simple explanation?'

'If there was I'm still waiting to hear it.'

'We went into the Mocha,' said Judith at once.

'The Mocha?' said her father.

'You know it,' said her mother, 'it's that dreadful place near the Ritz that has dance music blaring out until all hours.'

'Of course I know it. I treated a boy with a cut hand there one Saturday.'

'It's only a coffee bar,' said Judith. 'It's got a juke box, but they don't dance.'

'Don't they? Naturally I've never been inside,' said Mrs. Wilson.

The doctor coughed. 'Noisy place. Not very pleasant on a Saturday evening, I'd have thought.'

'We just wanted some coffee. It was near, and it was open.'

'I expect it's still open,' said her mother. 'We should be thankful you didn't stay any longer.' She looked at her husband.

'The thing is, Judith,' he said after an uncomfortable pause, 'we think you're a little young.'

She waited.

'— to go out with Tom by yourself,' he went on as though there had been no break.

She waited again.

'And we'd rather you didn't do it any more,' he finished.

Now it had been said for her, Mrs. Wilson felt free to elaborate. 'Of course if Mark goes too it's different. But you and Tom are just not old enough to behave responsibly. You had your chance and look what happened.' Judith's silence drove her on. 'An hour and a half late home and not a word of apology.'

'I'm sorry.'

'After you'd promised!' continued her mother uncontrollably. Her father made a small silencing gesture.

'Good-night,' said Judith, and went up to bed.

8

Mrs. Devenish and Mrs. Wilson sat drinking coffee while Jonathan tried to explore beneath the living-room sideboard.

'He's not very keen on the playpen since he started crawling.'

'I don't remember when mine rebelled . . . One forgets so much. It's rather sad.'

'At any rate he can't reach very high yet. Something's safe if it's on the seat of a chair.' Mrs. Wilson couldn't help noticing that this was no mere figure of speech; most of the chairs in the room had things on their seats. 'We'll all have to be much tidier as soon as he learns to stand.'

'Of course when one starts to be able to reason with them . . .'

'Hugh thinks he should understand No already. He's been giving him lessons.'

Jonathan began to scream.

'He gets stuck,' said Mrs. Devenish, going to the rescue. Wiping his nose she sat him down in the middle of his toys. He took hold of a rubber cube and examined it with a face of concentration.

'I quite envy you him.'

'But you wouldn't want the other four?'

'Oh gracious, the mere prospect makes me feel weak. Frankly I don't know how you cope.'

'Nor do I.' Mrs. Devenish glanced vaguely round the room and wondered for a moment if she had ever achieved a level of housekeeping constantly fit for unexpected callers. She believed not.

'Babies are so easy somehow,' said Mrs. Wilson. Mrs. Devenish thought of the nappies. 'But as for children I sometimes think the older they get the more worry they are. Look at this business with Judith.'

'I shouldn't let it bother you too much. I expect it'll sort itself out.'

'What does bother me is how it could all have happened without my noticing. I knew the four of them were going round together quite a lot and I was rather pleased; Judith never used to get on with Mark, and I was glad they were growing out of that. If I hadn't been busy with my last book I'd have paid more attention. Then perhaps I wouldn't have been so taken by surprise. It's made me feel I don't know where I am at all.'

'You don't think you might be imagining more than really exists?'

'Not judging from the way Judith's reacted. When we said it must stop she didn't say a word, and she hasn't since; and that's unlike her.'

'Though I suppose nothing quite like this has happened before.'

'Well no,' said Mrs. Wilson a trifle impatiently. 'Once is enough. Oh dear, and it's not as though I haven't always been perfectly friendly to Tom.'

A little hard, thought Mrs. Devenish, to expect Tom to repay friendliness by showing none himself.

'If she wanted to pick one of Mark's friends, why couldn't it be someone like Kim Welwyn?'

'He's at the technical college now, isn't he? I think Polly's mentioned his name.'

'I believe he is, yes.'

'I didn't know he was a friend of Mark's.'

'Well, not a close friend, but he was in the same class and I used to meet him on speech days and occasions like that. He's the kind of boy that gets chosen to carry the sandwiches round. Very presentable . . . I can't help feeling he'd have managed to keep things light. Tom's as broody as Judith. They came in the other week hand in hand, and his tie matched her dress (it seems she made it for him) and one could feel it all round them. A sort of miasma.'

The characters in Mrs. Wilson's books did not have miasmal emotions. Mrs. Devenish put her choice of words down to her anxiety. She seemed to regret it herself, giving her shoulders a little shake and asking in a different tone: 'How is Polly getting on?'

'At the tech? It seems to be working fairly well. She found it all a bit bewildering at first; then she seemed to be settling quite nicely, but lately she's been rather moody again.'

'It is her ordinary level year, isn't it.'

'I don't think that's the trouble; she could worry a bit more about her exams without harm. No, I believe it's this lecturer who taught them at school last year. She takes special care with her appearance on his days, and she comes in either elated or thoroughly depressed. She's writing a novel because he encouraged the idea; she spends hours on it nearly every evening.'

'That all sounds very innocent,' said Mrs. Wilson with a slightly wistful smile.

'A bit irksome for the rest of us, though.'

'Do you think she regrets leaving school at all?'

'She doesn't seem to; she's quite enthusiastic about the tech. The boys sound very lively, and she's made a fairly close friend of one girl, Liz. She had her home to tea. Really a rather extraordinary person, but likeable under it all.'

'What, the makeup?'

'That among other things – yes, as for makeup you can't imagine. I felt rather sorry for her actually, she looked so – but I didn't feel at all sorry for Polly when she came in looking the same . . . She'd been with Garth to *Lollipop Boy*.'

'Judith saw them. I wondered if you knew.'

'Not until afterwards. I wasn't best pleased.'

'I can imagine. I suppose he'd persuaded her into it.'

'Oh it was six of one and half a dozen of the other, I'm sure. I don't think they'll be tempted to repeat it; I gathered it was rather a fiasco.'

There was an outburst of screams from Jonathan, who had got stuck again under the sideboard.

'He's just about ready for his rest,' said Mrs. Devenish, jogging him in her arms while he continued to cry.

'And I must go. Lovely to see you; you must drop in on me next time. Good-bye, you poppet.' She put her face close to the baby's red one. 'It really is the best age,' she said with unabated conviction.

One evening later that week Judith came. Although the bulb in the attic had just failed Polly dragged up an electric fire and they crouched on the floor in front of it, their shadows enormous in the rosy glow. The nearest street lamp outlined in gleaming detail the frame of the new curtainless window; the skylight over their heads was a dead black square.

'And now we can only go if Mark comes along to take care of us,' said Judith. Her eyes were in shadow about the uniform ruddiness of her cheeks and lips.

'Blimey, that's a bit much.'

'Yes.'

'What does Mark think about it?'

'I hope he doesn't know.'

'You won't ask him next time?'

'I'm not begging him to be a chaperon. And he won't want to come if you don't.'

'Oh bother! I suppose all this is my fault.'

'I didn't mean it like that,' said Judith quickly. 'It isn't really anybody's fault. Nobody could have guessed Ma'd get so hysterical.'

'No. She's usually so calm.'

'At least she hasn't said I must stop seeing him. Next time he comes round I shall just have to try and explain the cinema rule somehow.'

'Haven't you seen him since it happened?'

'No.' The single word echoed in a melancholy

way. 'I think he might be feeling scared. He's always a bit shy with Ma, and missing the last bus did make me rather late. He could have guessed there'd be some kind of row. I would have rung him up, but he's not on the telephone; and I don't quite like to go to his house when he hasn't asked me. Mark's been, but I never have.'

'Can't you get Mark to ferret him out?'

'No. I can't.'

'Oh well, goodness me.' It upset Polly to hear her so forlorn. 'I know, you'd better all come here and help with my room this Saturday. I can ask Tom myself when I see him tomorrow. The thing is I really don't want to spend money on the cinema or anything like that at the moment because I'm saving up for my party, and anyway the room *has* got to be finished, and what with homework it doesn't leave much time for going out. How would that be?'

'Fine,' said Judith, laughing at her vehemence.

'I expect I'll have to ask Garth as well,' mused Polly. 'He's been getting sulkier and sulkier on the phone. I don't think he really believes in this room at all.'

'Is your party certain yet?'

'I think so. Mummy wouldn't quite say yes, but after the way she reacted when I asked her she can't really say no either.'

'Who will you invite?'

'Oh. Well.' Polly settled into a new position and clasped her ankles. 'All of us, of course – that's you and me and Mark and Tom, oh and Garth. Then

Liz from tech, and I thought Dad and Sandy and Boris as well. And Kim.'

'Three girls and seven boys,' said Judith after a moment.

'Bordigals,' said Polly, 'you're right. I hadn't noticed.'

'Equal numbers aren't essential, I suppose.'

'No, but three to seven's going too far. What other girls do I know? Batty. I'll ask Batty.'

'I should think she'd like that. Aren't there any others at the tech? If Kim's coming, how about Louise?'

'I'm not having *Louise*.'

'One of the others, then?'

'Kim can manage without Louise for one evening, I should hope.'

'Or don't you talk to anyone except Liz?'

'It's not as though they were a proper pair.'

'There's always school people . . . Jane or Melody – you once went to a party of Cynthia's, didn't you?'

'It was Humphrey's party as well, so I'd have to have them both,' said Polly, diverted. 'Which would leave the numbers just as uneven. In any case I certainly wouldn't ask Cynthia. Or Melody, or Jane.' She sighed. 'I suppose it will have to be Louise. At least she's dry.'

'You mean trained?' asked Judith gravely.

'I mean she doesn't make me want to wring her out.' She shifted her position again. 'Ouch. Are you getting splinters? Let's go down and have a hot drink.'

She jumped to her feet. Judith unplugged the fire and followed.

Polly had found, one lunchtime, some sale price curtain material, extravagantly patterned in murky blues and greens with bright peacock eyes. Her mother, persuaded to look at it next time she was shopping, said it was still very expensive; sighed, supposed whatever they got would cost about the same, and agreed that Polly could buy it on Saturday morning. It was the first thing she showed Judith in the afternoon.

'Shall we start making the curtains?'

'I thought we might. We can use the machine.'

Judith fingered the edge of the material. 'It'll be nice to work with. Did you get matching thread?'

'I forgot,' said Polly, dismayed.

'Let's go and see if your mother has any that'll do.'

They found a reel which matched reasonably well. Polly had forgotten rings too, but Judith didn't think they'd get far enough to need them that afternoon. Tom offered to put up curtain rods and also shelves; a few minutes' talk convinced Mr. Devenish that he knew what he was doing, and he handed over the necessary tools with scarcely a twinge. Mark chose to sand the floorboards; a job requiring more muscles and less skill. Polly was just measuring the window when Garth arrived.

Hugh had let him in; 'another of Polly's friends,' he told his mother, bored. 'I sent him up.'

'Is this where you are?' called Garth, climbing uncertainly up the second flight of stairs.

'Oh, you came! Good,' said Polly.

'I said I would, didn't I?'

'Yes, but you didn't sound very keen.'

He looked round, surprised to find the others there. 'Hallo,' said Judith, echoed by Tom. Mark said nothing.

Garth walked up and down. 'Mind,' said Judith, who was spreading the curtain material on clean newspaper at the opposite end of the floor from Mark.

'Oh sorry.'

'Do you like the room?' asked Polly.

Mark began sanding ferociously. Garth, raising his voice, said that he did. 'Though it's a bit difficult to tell while it's so bare.'

'It soon won't be,' said Polly briskly.

'Is that curtain stuff? It's very splendid. What kind of carpet will you have?'

'I shan't. I might have a rug by the bed, but I want the floor to show. When it's been sanded we're going to put polyurethane on.'

'I see.' He continued to wander, idly examining the debris of decoration stacked round the walls.

'If you want something to do you might move some of that stuff out of my way,' grunted Mark without pausing in his exertions. His face was flushed, and a lock of hair clung to his forehead. Tom worked more placidly, whistling as he used the screwdriver; he liked this kind of job.

'Where shall I move it to?' Garth asked, cradling an unsteady pile of paint tins in his arms.

'Oh anywhere,' said Polly through a mouthful of pins. 'Put it on the bit Mark's done.'

'He doesn't seem to have done very much yet.'

'Perhaps you'd like to see if you can go any faster,' snapped Mark, sitting back on his heels.

'I only meant there wasn't room.'

'Put it on the landing then,' said Polly impatiently.

After several trips up and down Garth asked: 'What are you going to have on the walls?'

'You mean apart from paint?'

'He probably expects tapestries,' muttered Mark.

'Are you going to have any pictures?'

'I hadn't thought.'

'Bring out the old masters,' said Tom cheerfully.

'I think you can get travel posters free,' said Judith.

'Mm.' Polly was dubious.

'I'll do you a mural on here if you like.' Garth waved a piece of plywood two foot square.

'Good God!' said Mark; and Tom snorted with laughter.

'I just thought it would use up all the left-over paint.' Garth put the wood down again.

'Yes, why not?' said Polly. 'Let's see how it turns out.'

'You can have this newspaper,' said Judith, gathering up the curtains. 'We've finished with it now.'

'Oh to work on, do you mean? Thank you,' said Garth.

'Work,' echoed Mark silently with an expressive glance at Tom.

The two girls went downstairs to the sewing machine. The attic was beginning to feel crowded;

Polly thought it a good thing she'd decided not to ask Liz as well. Liz hadn't come to tea again yet, but Polly had been to her house and met her brothers: Robert, a sulky boy of twelve, and James, a boisterous four-year-old who had played bus conductors round Polly's chair and somewhat embarrassed her by shouting 'Ding ding! Minja bosoms, lady!' at the top of his voice.

'Is Tom up to date on your parents?' Polly asked Judith.

'I told him on the way here.'

'Did he mind?'

'He said it was just one of those things.' To Tom, parents had a right to be irrational; Judith needn't have worried. She felt now she would have preferred him to be at least a little indignant. 'Apparently his father often has rows with his sister about her boy friends.' ('And about her leaving the basin stopped up when she washes her hair,' Tom had said.)

'Older sister?'

'Yes, she's nearly nineteen.'

Polly had been sceptical when Judith said they wouldn't need curtain rings that day, but as usual she was right.

'Making things always takes longer than you think.'

The boys had done better; by the time Mrs. Devenish, who was providing tea in relays, asked if they'd all like to come down their jobs were on the point of completion. Garth's mural was a whirly abstract in orange, white and midnight blue: Polly's chosen colour scheme. She recoiled a little from the great wet square and said 'It will certainly go...'

'Do you think you'll use it, then?'

She decided the colours looked even better stirred up together. 'Yes. Thank you. I say, those shelves are good.'

'Floor's all right too,' said Tom.

Polly bent down to feel. 'Oh lovely. Like the insides of your legs when you've been walking in wet wellingtons.'

'Whose legs?' asked Tom, a trifle alarmed.

'You wouldn't know. You wear trousers.' This for some reason made them all giggle.

'I bet old Mark's arms are aching,' said Tom as they went downstairs.

'It's nothing.'

'Mine are,' said Garth.

'The paint was so heavy,' sighed Mark.

Garth ignored this. 'It's the concentration.'

'You mean you weren't doing it with your eyes closed?'

Polly suppressed a smile and thanked Mark for finishing the whole floor. She wished Garth got on better with the others; it never seemed to work when they mixed.

Food and drink smoothed their differences for a while.

'How's Louise?' asked Judith.

'Still coming to English. That girl's got determination; she and Mr. Routledge don't like each other a bit. She said she'd misplaced her book one day and he said "D'you mean you've lost it Miss Mannering?" '

'It must be funny to be called Miss.'

'He calls me Polly – the other lecturers don't, though. He even calls Liz Liz. But Sandy's Sanders and Dad's Alsop. He once saw Louise and Dad walking up together and he keeps teasing them about it – Dad wrote about somebody that he wasn't much enamoured of something, and Mr. Routledge said "You must have got that from Miss Mannering. It's the Mannering style. I expect it sounds lovely when you're whispering sweet nothings in each other's ears" . . . It's really a bit unfair to Dad.'

'Who's Dad?' asked Mark.

'The one with warts,' said Garth to Polly's surprise; he must have paid more attention to her talk about the tech than she'd realized.

'I know Louise is Kim Welwyn's number one girl,' said Mark, not to be outdone.

'Dad's warts are gone,' said Polly quickly.

'Did he have them cut out?' asked Tom. Obviously he hadn't heard about charming by post; just as well; Polly didn't think her conscience would have let her accept a postal order from him.

'They simply went,' she said. Really she had no reason to feel guilty. Dad was very pleased about his cure, and had announced that he would recommend it to two friends, apprentices doing the O.N.C. course. Polly had received a small bunch of letters just when she thought there would be no more.

Hugh came in and looked at the table. 'Does anyone want that piece of cake?' he asked.

'Yes. Go away,' said Polly and passed it to Tom, who hadn't had any yet.

'I say, I hear you're writing a book,' said Judith.

'However could you hear that?'

'Your mother told mine.'

'Oh.' Polly still felt ruffled.

'Are you really writing one?'

'Sort of.'

'It's not a proper story,' said Hugh from the corner. 'It just goes on and on about Kirn.'

For a moment Polly couldn't speak.

'It's boring,' said Hugh.

'You absolute little *horror*.' Polly ground back her chair and Hugh fled, shouting 'Sorry' as he went through the door.

'I suppose it wasn't meant for children?' said Mark, as Polly sat down again.

'No, it wasn't.'

'You never told me you were writing something,' said Garth.

'It wasn't meant for anyone.'

'Is Curne the chap's surname?' asked Tom.

Thinking of her escape Polly forgot to answer. Easy to misread Kim as Kirn if one had never encountered it before.

'No I shan't. You must take care of yourself,' said the voice of Mrs. Devenish from the kitchen.

'But I said sorry!'

'You had no business reading it in the first place.'

'He seems to think you'll murder him,' said Mark with a tentative smile.

'So I might.'

'Give him what for,' advised Tom.

'Oh, he's impossible. My room's going to need a lock on the door.'

'Or maybe just a sort of automatic guillotine that drops on him if he touches the cupboards.'

'I don't think I'd get planning permission for that,' said Polly.

9

'I'm longing to see your loft,' said Liz.

She and Polly had a classroom to themselves and were sitting on the windowsill with their legs hanging outside.

'It doesn't look like a loft any more,' said Polly.

'But I do think you might ask Mr. Norris.' It was the sixth time she had thought so that day.

'He'd feel silly being the only lecturer.'

'You could have Mr. Routledge to keep him company. You've got a soft spot for him, haven't you?'

'Only in his proper place. Not at my party.'

'I'd like Mr. Norris in an improper place,' exclaimed Liz, flinging wide her arms. Then she sighed. 'Oh Polly, you may laugh, but really my dearest wish is for him to ask me out.'

'No,' said Polly thoughtfully. 'I wouldn't laugh at that.'

'Ah, what the hell! Maybe they will one day.'

There was a moment when Polly could have pretended to think Liz was still talking about Mr Routledge. She allowed it to pass in silence.

'You don't mind me knowing?' said Liz urgently.

'No. It's all right.'

'I'm sure nobody else has guessed. The only reason I did was . . .' She paused to consider.

'Because of your woman's intuition.'

'Something like that.'

'There was a girl at my school who had woman's intuition. Melody, her name was. She had a boy friend called Roger who wrote to her every day.' Lighter in spirits Polly swung her legs. 'That's the lecturers' car park down there, isn't it? I hope nobody comes by.'

'They probably wouldn't look up. Unless we threw something, of course.'

'"*Er – Miss Cartwright – I think you've dropped your shoe*",' said Polly. 'Actually this sun's not quite good enough for sitting. Let's go for a walk.'

'All right,' said Liz amiably. 'I expect the exercise'll do us good.' She took her coat from the pegs. 'Are you leaving all your stuff?'

'I'd better take my money I suppose.' Polly opened her case. Her purse had buried itself in the loose papers that collected like dead leaves at the bottom. Some escaped and drifted to the floor; she bundled them back and snapped the catches. Liz opened the door and a gale howled across the room.

'Ought we to shut that window?' said Polly as scraps of litter whirled past their ankles.

'Don't let's bother.'

They went downstairs and out of the main doors. Liz turned towards the shops but Polly said: 'Let's go the other way. We can explore the park, the one we see from the canteen.'

The park believed in simplicity. It had tall trees and stretches of springy turf, kept down by children's feet; swings and a sand pit. There was a sharp spicy autumnal smell in the air.

'Nice. I've been meaning to come here all term,' said Polly.

They weren't the only students taking advantage of the day's unusual warmth. A group of boys were kicking a ball on the grass, and a smaller group walked past the girls, one nodding to Liz.

'Hallo,' she said with a bright empty smile, and to Polly after he'd gone: 'Keeps pestering me to go to Saturday nights at his youth club. Just because I sometimes dance with him after lunch.'

'You do go out with some boys, don't you?'

'Of course. I'm not going into *retirement* on Mr. Norris's account. Why? Don't you?'

'I suppose I do sort of.'

'My, that sounds ominous.'

'No; just a bit of a bore.'

'Oh boring, I'll grant you. Find me a boy who isn't and I expect I'd forget Norris just like that.' She snapped her fingers. 'Your charmer looks as though he might not be.'

'He's not mine,' said Polly.

'They will talk about the last time they got drunk.' Liz made retching noises. 'How they had to poke at the bits of carrot to make them go down the drain.'

'Liz, no!' Polly felt rather like retching herself.

'Only now if they start I say: I don't want to hear how you had to poke the bits, etcetera – and that usually shuts them up.'

'I should think it would.'

They were walking close to the swings. Small children sailed to and fro while their mothers, when not required to push, chatted on a nearby bench.

Words written on the undersides of the seats appeared in flashes too brief for comprehension; although they might be better hidden it was tantalizing. When one swing was vacated Polly stepped forward and seized it, but changed her mind at the last moment and sat on top instead.

'Want a push?' offered Liz.

'No, I can do it.' She hadn't for years, but it wasn't a thing one could forget. She slipped effortlessly into the old routine, thrusting higher and higher, feeling the pull in her stomach muscles and the rush of wind through her hair. The swings had been sited by someone with imagination, right at the top of a long grassy slope; she could see clear across to the far horizon, and in between were all the roofs of Stilwell. Each time she came forward the ground dropped away and there was nothing but sky, blueness and cloud and birds calling. She felt she was on equal terms with the birds; flying couldn't be much better than this.

She might have gone on for ever if it hadn't been for the shout.

'Polly!'

Leave me alone, she thought.

'Poll-y! Hey Polly, come back!'

It was Kim. Immediately her arms sagged and she came down, down and down, slower and slower, back to the dull old ground. The rut of worn soil centred beneath her and she slid to her feet with a rattle of chains, scarcely noticing the untidy queue of children who waited with smudged reproachful faces just behind Kim.

'Earthbound,' he said.

She nodded.

'You know,' he remarked conversationally, 'I always used to think being potbound was something that happened to babies.'

I don't believe a word of it, she thought.

'Rather like hens being eggbound.'

A small bubble of laughter escaped her. She completely forgot Liz, who had melted away in a tactful manner and was not going to reappear for some time.

'Do you want a turn?'

'It would scarcely be fair to the little ones. Besides, I might break it. You didn't need to worry about that.'

'Oh —' (she hadn't even thought of it) 'but surely they make them far stronger than they need to be. They wouldn't be safe otherwise.'

'There's something very shaky about your logic.' He was laughing at her. She looked up at him; not exactly broad, but a good head taller, he probably would weigh quite a bit more than her. His dark curly hair and natural high colour made handsome the only word for him. In her view this wasn't exactly a compliment, but she liked the good-humoured way he accepted his looks.

'What's the going rate for thoughts?' he asked, aware of her interest.

Her presence of mind scattered. 'Dunno.'

'Sixpence?'

'I've stopped thinking them now,' she said more firmly.

There was a felled tree trunk lying embedded in the grass. Without consulting each other they sat down. 'Cigarette?' said Kim. 'Oh no, I remember, you aren't allowed to.'

But he forgot she didn't choose to. She said. 'You can't see the college at all from here.'

'We could spend the afternoon and nobody would know. Only then you'd miss Mr. Routledge.'

Could he have been discussing her with Louise? Her face stiffened.

'That is, he'd miss you. You're rather his blue-eyed girl, aren't you?'

'We have a working arrangement,' said Polly quickly. 'He leaves me alone and I work.' Although he smiled she sensed that Kim's mood wasn't altogether light. She changed the subject.

'Kim, I'm having a party in two weeks' time . . .'

'End of term.'

'Is it? Oh yes. Well this is a sort of room-warming party, and I wondered, would you like to come?'

'Thank you very much.'

He hadn't said yes, did he mean yes?'

'What room are we going to warm?'

He must mean yes. 'Mine in the roof,' she said, and explained.

'So – privacy at last,' he commented.

'I need it. The kids have even started reading my diary.'

'That must be quite a hazard.' *Yes*, she nearly said, *it's mostly about you*. 'Still, you seem to have obliging parents. I take it they'll be there, the night of the party?'

'Mine's rather a large family to turn out.' The thought had crossed her mind, only to be dismissed.

'I'll look forward to meeting them all.'

'The children,' said Polly firmly, 'will be keeping out of the way.'

'You must be an expert on children.'

'I need to be.'

'We've got one in the house at the moment; belonging to my aunt and uncle. They're staying for a week.'

'A he or a she?'

'She. Causes all sorts of unexpected problems. I came in last Saturday when they'd all gone to bed: crept upstairs with my usual care, switched off the landing light, and then this little voice squeaked at me to put it back on because she couldn't sleep without it. "Oh," I said, "you must be a light sleeper"; which didn't amuse her at all, but I in my alcoholic state found it so funny I woke the whole house.'

Picturing Kim helpless on the landing, Polly wondered if this was the moment at which Liz would use her remark about carrots.

'That reminds me – where is Liz?' she said suddenly.

'Was she here?'

'She was before I went on the swing.'

'Maybe she got tired of waiting.'

Feeling a little guilty Polly looked at her watch. 'I suppose we ought to be getting back.'

Kim stubbed out his cigarette and rose, offering her a hand. She was up before she noticed; she turned away and made fists inside her pockets, angry at the lost chance.

'Is Louise getting an invitation?' he asked as they walked.

'Yes,' said Polly, and wished she had made it no.

'You've known her some time, haven't you?'

'I've never counted it up.'

She wondered if her party would be alcoholic enough for Kim. She had abandoned her original idea of wine for three reasons: it would cost too much, she was pretty sure her mother wouldn't be keen on it, and she didn't really like it. She was going to buy a small quantity and use it in a recipe she had found for fruit cup; her wart-charming money would cover the necessary ingredients.

They found the classroom almost full. Liz had kept a seat for Polly, and Louise had one for Kim.

'I am sorry,' Polly began.

'Don't worry. I came back with Hilary and Jackie.'

Kim was describing the park. 'You should have come.'

'It sounds awfully healthy,' replied Louise with wrinkled nose.

Mr. Routledge entered. Their homework had been to write a short scene illustrating squalor; 'Alsop, read yours aloud,' he said.

Dad found the place. 'It was dark,' he began laboriously. 'Somebody had smashed the street light. The pavement was knee deep in rubbish. There was a dead cat in the gutter. The dark street strank, I mean stank, of the Gents. Bacteria could be seen everywhere . . .'

Mr. Routledge closed his eyes for a moment, then held up a hand as Dad's voice continued inaudibly.

'Just a minute, Alsop. Wait for the laughter to subside.'

'It isn't meant to be funny,' protested Dad. 'They can see them with microscopes anyway, can't they sir?'

'No, your main character's got D.T.s,' said Sandy. 'He thinks a crowd of great white bugs is crawling out of the cat. He's trying to run but he can't get through the rubbish . . .'

'There aren't any characters,' said Dad.

'What about those smelly gents? One of them's a policeman with a microscope —'

'Sanders,' said Mr. Routledge wearily, 'are there any more at home like you?'

'Ooh none like me, sir.'

Mr. Routledge didn't ask to hear about anyone else's squalor. He wanted to talk about letters.

'If you never write anything else, you'll write them,' he said. 'Some of them will be important, so you may as well learn to make a good impression. Too many people can't write a literate letter, and that includes most of those whose business it is to produce them.' Small wonder so few of the secretaries still attended his lectures, Polly thought. 'You can't make up for lack of grammar with a sprinkling of business terms.'

'Can you give us an example, sir?' asked Louise.

'Don't you know what I mean, Miss Mannering?'

'No sir,' said Louise politely.

'I'm sure Polly does. Well, I picked up quite a good example in the corridor just now.' He spread a crumpled footmarked piece of paper in front of him, frowned at it and said: 'Written by A. B. Potts

– no Potts in the room, is there? In any case it's scarcely his property any longer. And it begins Dear Sir, which doesn't give much clue to the present owner. "Dear Sir, re your ad in the Stilwell Herald the fourteenth of inst and see you do warts charming. I have, in all sixteen warts on my hands which at sixpence a wart I make, eight shillings. Please find enclosed postal order for which amount and oblidge . . ." '

Polly was sitting right under his nose. He noticed the great start she gave, just as he had noticed her involuntary nod a few minutes earlier. Forgetting Louise he leaned forward.

'I beg your pardon, Polly,' he said, 'surely it isn't yours?'

'Not – not exactly.' Sandy was staring at her, and so was Dad.

'Your name's not A. B. Potts. Or Sir either.'

'No sir.'

'Well look, do you want it?' He held it out. 'If you did write it your inventive powers are even better than I thought.'

He obviously wished to be rid of it; he had caught her embarrassment, and she couldn't now pretend it had nothing to do with her. She took it.

'Right,' he said, 'all get ready to write one of your own.'

Polly was very subdued for the rest of the hour. She had pinned the horrible letter under a book, and her eyes kept wandering back to it.

'So what was all that about?' said Liz directly Mr. Routledge had gone. Polly shook her head.

'I don't get it,' complained Dad as she tore the dogeared paper in four and dropped it into the bin. 'Has she got warts?'

'No, she charms 'em,' said Boris laconically.

Sandy looked as if he would like to believe it but couldn't quite. 'You don't, do you?' he asked directly.

There was no help for it. 'Yes,' said Polly.

'Polly!' said Liz.

'Was it you put the ad in the paper, then?' asked Sandy.

'Yes. I never thought anyone I knew would answer it, though.' She risked a look at Dad. It was not returned.

'But where did you find out how to do the charming?' asked Sandy.

'Oh, I didn't do anything. At least, I mean —' (though staring at his hands, Dad was obviously listening) '—the idea was, if people believed their warts would go, then they would.'

'And they did,' said Sandy, also looking at Dad's hands.

'How enterprising of you,' said Kim.

'I suppose that was why you never let on even when Dad said he'd answered the ad,' said Sandy, following his own train of thought. 'I mean, if he'd known it was only you he probably wouldn't have been able to believe hard enough.' He gave Dad a nudge. 'Would you?'

Dad cast one bemused look at Polly and said nothing. Certainly she had never considered telling him the truth; not for Sandy's reason, ingenious though that was, but because she had been sure it would be impossibly embarrassing. As it was.

'Did you get many replies?' asked Kim.

'Not really. Enough to pay for my party.' She seized on this opportunity to change the subject. 'I'm hoping you'll all be able to come. Saturday fortnight.'

Boris and Sandy accepted.

'Wake up,' said Sandy to Dad, 'you've just been asked to a party.'

'Do you think you can come?' said Polly.

'A party? Well. Yes.' Dad's gaze shifted from her to Sandy. 'If you two are.' But at least he had looked her in the eye and accepted. She felt a little better.

'Am I included?' asked Louise.

'Of course,' said Polly, matching her civilized tone. 'Kim's coming.'

'I think I can manage it,' said Louise. 'I'll check and let you know.'

They moved off to the canteen, piecing together the full story of the warts on the way. Kim thought it remarkably neat.

'Whatever will you do next!' said Liz.

'One hardly likes to think,' murmured Louise, and turned to Dad. 'Will I have the pleasure of your company on the bus tonight?'

He made an inaudible reply.

'You're very quiet,' said Sandy to Tom. 'Going to gets yours charmed now, are you eh?'

'I expect so,' he said vaguely.

'Well cheer up. You look like a wet week.'

Tom said: 'What's a blue-backed six-legged

kerbstone . . . I mean: what's got a blue back and six legs and eats kerbstones? . . . I've spoilt it, I'm afraid.'

'You have, haven't you!' said Kim.

They started getting their tea. Tom and Polly were last.

'Let's take ours over there,' he said, indicating a far corner. He had more of a battered hangdog look than he usually got from one failed joke.

'Right,' said Polly. Louise had already detached Kim, and Dad had joined a table of unfamiliar faces, all of whom for some reason seemed to be looking in her direction. When they saw she had noticed they stopped.

'Has Judith told you,' said Tom, stirring his tea round and round.

'She hasn't told me anything recently.'

'She's packed me up.'

'Oh Tom, no!'

He nodded miserably.

'I don't believe it.'

'She has.'

'But she can't mean it.'

'She said it.'

'Her parents must have made her.' Polly thought for a moment. 'Could they be that mad?'

'No, it's her – it's Judith – it's not them.'

Polly was silenced. They drank their tea.

'Just thought I'd tell you,' said Tom.

'Yes. Gosh. I'm awfully sorry.' She felt inadequate. She had come to like Tom very much, and more, to like him and Judith as a pair. One of her daydreams was of herself and Kim making another pair, and the four of them going out together. She could never have felt for Tom what Judith did (he obviously appealed to her maternal instincts and there wasn't much maternal about Polly) but nor had she thought Judith would ever change. Or at least not in the foreseeable future.

'Did you have a quarrel?' she asked, groping for reasons.

'Oh no.'

No, they never had quarrelled. It would probably be very hard to quarrel with Tom; he'd simply fail to co-operate. Another reason why he wouldn't do for her.

'She just said . . . she said . . . she didn't think we should see each other any more. With things the way they were.'

'You mean with her mother? But then that does sound as though she was pushed into it, Tom.'

'No. It was her idea.'

She supposed he should know. They were silent again until she said: 'There goes Liz. I'd better, too.'

'The boys aren't bothering.'

'They don't when it's only Norris, they've been getting later and later; but Liz won't like it if I join in.'

Liz had already begun to fret when Polly reached the classroom. None of the boys was there. 'Rotten lot,' she said. 'He told them about it last time *and* the time before.'

'He just makes them worse,' said Polly.

'They make themselves worse. They're seeing how far they can go. It's mean.'

Mr. Norris came in. 'Good afternoon . . . where are the others?' he asked.

'In the canteen,' said one of the girls.

'They'll be here in a minute, sir,' said Liz.

But they weren't. The electric clock dropped minutes one after another into an invisible bucket; Liz chewed her lip and Mr. Norris sat fidgeting with his papers.

'I'm going to call the register,' he said abruptly.

He did so, leaving a pause after each unanswered name. He was collecting the homework when the boys came trooping in. They sat down, carefree and flushed with laughter.

'You haven't closed the door,' said Mr. Norris. Boris got up and closed it.

'It may interest you to know you were all marked absent at ten past three.' His voice shook slightly.

There was a rumble of surprised apology, drowning the comment by one that if they'd been marked absent they needn't bother to stay.

'If it happens again you'll go before Dr. Makepiece.'

'We go before him at four o'clock,' murmured Sandy.

'Leave it. *Leave* it,' Liz commanded her ink bottle.

'I beg your pardon, Miss Cartwright?'

'Oh – er – nothing, sir.'

'Then don't interrupt.'

Liz, speechless, blushed very thoroughly all over her face.

'Getting tough,' said Sandy after he'd gone.

'Yes,' said Boris.

Dad announced a decision. 'I'm not going to be late next time.'

'Not even a little tiny bit?' said Sandy. 'Well well well.'

'Are you?' asked Dad suspiciously.

'I'm not stupid.'

'He's *changed*,' breathed Liz to Polly.

'Who, Norris? He needed to.'

'Oh yes I know, but he's *different*.'

'Better or worse?'

'I'm not sure,' said Liz with a faraway look.

When Polly got home she found a letter waiting from Penelope Batts. 'Batty can come,' she told her mother. 'That makes everybody, if Louise isn't otherwise engaged.' On the last words she sniffed.

They talked about food; Polly planned a buffet supper half-way through. She had made a list.

'Rather a lot,' said her mother.

'I'll do all the cooking. Nearly everything can be got ready before; it's only things like the soup that need to be hot.'

'Do you think the guests will share your passion for tinned tomato soup?'

'I don't see why not. I know Mark and Judith like it. The point is the mugs; it makes a gorgeous drink, just right with sausages on sticks. Judith's going to lend me some mugs.'

'Has she asked her mother?'

'I'm sure she will.'

'Yes,' agreed Mrs. Devenish, thinking of Judith. Polly also thought of her, but in the context of Tom's news. She couldn't get over it. She decided to go round that Saturday.

She was forestalled in this by Judith, who came to visit her on Friday evening. The bulb in the attic had been replaced, though there wasn't much furniture yet; they sat on cushions on the pale shining floor.

'Good, isn't it?' said Polly. 'And you never have to polish it – just wipe it occasionally.'

'Very handy. I see you got the curtains finished.'

'Yes, the little one too. There was just enough stuff left to cover the cushions.'

The sliding curtain over the skylight had tasselled cords to pull it to and fro. 'They're off old dressing-gowns,' said Polly. 'I found them in the pieces bag.'

Judith wasn't really listening. 'How's Tom getting on with Mr. Routledge these days?' she asked.

'Oh, all right. I mean he's not much good, but Mr. Routledge likes him.'

'It doesn't always sound that way.'

'You should hear him with someone he doesn't like. Kim, say.'

'Why doesn't he like Kim?' asked Judith with a faint show of interest.

'I don't know. Perhaps he thinks he's conceited. The boys do.' ('What's he got to be so stuck up about?' Sandy had said. 'He may be doing A levels but he couldn't pass English.' 'I didn't pass either,' Tom had reminded them, and Boris had made one of his infrequent comments: 'You don't put on airs.')

'Is he better than Tom?'

'A bit, perhaps. I think he'd seem better even if he wasn't.' Polly decided Judith needed help. 'Tom's been talking to me.'

Judith turned to her quickly, her mouth open.

'He said you'd said you didn't want to see him any more.'

'Did he seem to mind?'

'Well, yes. Of course. What do you expect?'

'It wasn't that I didn't want to,' said Judith in an unhappy voice. 'I never told him that. It was because everything was getting so awful . . .'

'With your mother?'

'Yes. She wasn't letting us do anything. Polly, Tom came round one evening and he was going to help me with some maths; you know he often does. Mark had the television on so we started off in the other room, at the table, but Pa was there as well doing his income tax or something – he was much too engrossed to listen, but it made Tom all tongue-tied. So we went up in my room. Well . . . and then a few minutes later Ma came bursting in and ordered us downstairs. She was furious. Goodness knows what she thought we were doing. She didn't *say* anything, so we couldn't either, and Tom had to show me the maths downstairs and he was much too flustered to do it properly, and I had to keep saying I understood when we both knew I didn't. And it was all silly and horrible.'

'Yes,' said Polly, fairly well able to imagine.

'So we thought we'd try again another night. Tom said why didn't I come round to his house instead. He said we'd have to work downstairs because there's no table in his room but he wouldn't mind if I didn't, and his family would like to meet me. I didn't say anything beforehand because I thought my mother might make some nasty comment. I never expected – I mean, I don't ask for permission if I'm coming to see you, or Batty; I just say where I'm going as I leave. Only when I said I was going to Tom's she wouldn't let me.'

'But why?'

'I didn't ask. She'd only have said something awful. I know why, anyway. It's because she wanted me to go on being a child, and she thinks it's Tom's fault I'm not. And all he's done is be himself – but she never did like him much.' Judith paused. 'When I said he was expecting me she said I shouldn't have arranged it without asking. And you know he hasn't got a telephone, so I couldn't ring up and explain. In the end I persuaded Mark to go round, but he was awfully grumpy; I think it embarrassed him. He took Tom a letter.'

'Judith, you didn't say it in a letter?'

'No, I asked Tom to ring me. I gave him a time when I knew Ma wouldn't be in. But he's a bit hopeless on the phone; he'd probably have understood better if I had written it down.'

'Have you told your mother?'

'No, and I shan't. I won't have her thinking I've pushed Tom out.'

'Why not?' asked Polly, adding to herself, 'when you have?'

'Because she'd be pleased.' Judith's voice was always quiet, but it had a vicious note now that was new. 'I didn't do it to please her. I'd rather she thought Tom had got fed up; goodness knows he had reason.'

'I still don't see quite why you did do it,' admitted Polly.

'Nor does Mark. I thought you might.'

'Tom certainly doesn't. I reckoned maybe you didn't like him any more, but I see it isn't that.'

'No. It isn't that.'

'You don't know when you're lucky. The person you like may not always like you.'

'The person I like is Tom.' Judith's voice quivered and she looked away.

'Well, and do you expect him to go on liking you in a vacuum?' said Polly, exasperated. 'I don't think your mother being awkward is a good enough reason for chucking everything down the drain.'

Judith kept her face averted and spoke after a few minutes in a more normal voice. 'Did you mean . . . when you said that about liking a person, it sounded as though you meant yourself.'

'I suppose I did.' Polly had had time now to regret the impulse.

'I've been awfully obtuse. Is it Kim?'

'Bordigals, how did *you* know?' She realized her emphasis was rather rude. 'I mean, you haven't even seen us together.'

'You've talked about Kim,' said Judith apologetically. 'And Mark likes you, and Garth obviously does too, so it couldn't be either of them.'

Polly brushed Mark and Garth aside. 'What about the other tech boys?'

'They sound so young.'

'Well yes. They're all my age I suppose, and Kim's that bit older. You can have a proper conversation with him . . . about books, or films, or almost anything.'

Polly had grown used to discussing Kim only in

her diary, but Judith was a good listener and seemed to welcome the change of subject. 'And obviously Louise is more important to him than me,' she concluded several minutes later. 'That's why it seems such a waste, you and Tom off by yourselves and both miserable about it.'

'Tom is miserable, then?'

'Judith, yes. I told you.'

'He hasn't said anything.'

'How could he after what you said? You know he's not one to fight back. I thought that was what you liked about him.'

'I just like him. Do you think he thinks I don't?'

'He must wonder.'

'I'm sure I explained on the telephone . . . Oh well.' She sighed. 'At least I'll see him at your party.'

10

'I don't know that I'll go to Polly's party,' said Tom.

'What?' said Mark, horrified.

The two boys were walking along an asphalt footpath beside a railway cutting. Below them signal lights gleamed in the darkness. They would have been sitting in Tom's warm living-room but for the wish to talk.

'If Judith's going,' said Tom, vaguely explanatory.

'But damn it, it's not Judith's party. Polly wants you, doesn't she?'

'I suppose so. She hasn't said.'

'She must, if she invited you!'

'I mean she hasn't said she didn't.'

'Well then.'

'Judith'll be there,' said Tom. 'And she doesn't want to see me.'

'Let her look the other way,' said Mark callously. 'Brace up, Tom! I'll need your support, you know.'

'Bit like old times, isn't it.'

'Us on one side and them on the other? I suppose it is.'

'Not quite the same, though.'

They reached a footbridge over the line.

'If we go this way we can cut back along Wilton Street. It'll make like a circle,' said Tom.

'Righto.'

The metal bridge rang beneath their heels. They pursued separate thoughts of the party until Mark said:

'Maybe neither of us should go. Leave them to stew in their own juice.'

Tom had been growing faintly optimistic; he didn't really think Judith would look the other way when they met. Neither did he want to offend Polly. 'Oh I don't know,' he said unwillingly.

They walked in silence again until Tom's street drew near.

'See our breath,' said Mark as they passed under a lamp-post. 'Cold enough for snow.'

'Mum should be making some tea. Let's hurry.'

'Are we going to the party or aren't we?' challenged Mark.

'Yes,' said Tom, feeling reckless.

'All right, yes it is.'

'One more thing,' said Mr. Routledge, 'and then it's Christmas.'

Christmas, thought Polly, who had forgotten it. Carols and cards and cooking and (a sobering aspect) no money for presents. Somehow she didn't think Dad would be recommending her to any more warty friends. Then she remembered she was working on the post this year. Good.

She gazed at the uncurtained classroom windows. The winter afternoons made them seem particularly large. Ghost lamps hung outside in the blue twilight, reflections of the electric lights within. They had a coldly cheerful look.

'No homework for me, is there. You needn't do any in the holidays. Have a good time,' said Mr. Routledge. 'Don't get over-excited, Sanders.'

'Same to you, sir,' retorted Sandy, dashing out of the room.

'I asked for that,' Mr. Routledge told Liz and Polly, who were being uncontrollably amused.

'Yes sir. Happy Christmas, sir.'

When Polly got home her mother said: 'I think you might be able to use the attic on Saturday after all.'

Two days earlier Polly had discovered to her utmost gloom that her mother's idea of the party was quite different from her own. Mrs. Devenish envisaged them playing Postman's Knock in the sitting-room, and had said categorically that if they danced over Jonathan's head they would wake him up.

'You can do your dancing downstairs if you're set against party games. Though I don't see why you shouldn't have both; they do help to break the ice.'

'They're childish,' Polly had said with disgust.

Her mother explained now: 'Mrs. Peabody's offered to have Jonathan.' The Peabodys lived next door. 'She caught me when I was – I mean we were talking when I was hanging the washing out. Apparently the younger ones told Jacko about the party and she remarked that if your friends were anything like Ken's wouldn't it be better if the baby slept with her?'

'What did you say?' demanded Polly.

'I haven't said anything yet. There's no denying it

would simplify matters, and she seemed very ready to have him . . .' Too ready, thought Polly, suspecting her mother had been slightly put off. 'And of course he does know her from her talking to him when he used to be out in the pram.'

'If he wasn't good he could always come back again,' said Polly. Actually she didn't see Mrs. Peabody relinquishing him for anything less than hour-long screams.

'I suppose so. But then it's a bit embarrassing that you haven't invited Ken.'

'Ken! ' said Polly, aghast. 'I couldn't have Ken. I haven't spoken to him for years.'

'No, I agree you haven't much in common. I don't suppose it would be his kind of party in any case.'

'I'm sure it wouldn't,' said Polly fervently. When her mother didn't reply she went on: 'Can Jonathan sleep there, then?'

'Well . . . yes, I should think so. If Mrs. Peabody hasn't thought better of it by now. You can go and see if you like.'

Polly went at once, and was able to complete the arrangements at the expense of half an hour's chat. The cot was to be taken next-door after Jonathan's rest on Saturday. Polly and Michael did it between them. Michael was quite good with a screwdriver.

'And you'd better dust our bedroom,' said Mrs. Devenish, 'if that's where they're going to leave their coats.'

'All right, but first I've got to go and buy the cherries for the top of the trifle.'

She found other last-minute things that needed

buying, including tights for herself. When she returned her mother was cleaning upstairs. She offered to take over.

'No, I'll carry on now I've started. You do something else.'

Polly went to begin the cheese straws. They were fun to do but rather fiddly.

'Are you still messing around with those?' asked her mother some while later. 'Time's getting on, you know.'

'Don't you think they look pretty?' She was arranging finished straws in bundles.

'Lovely, but they won't be very filling, will they.'

'Well, there are other things to fill people – the sausages, and the savoury flans.'

'The flans,' echoed her mother. 'I'd forgotten the flans. When are you going to do them?'

'Next. After I've just rung Judith and washed my hair.'

'Surely you washed it a couple of days ago?'

Polly stopped everything. 'Mummy, I can't possibly give a party with my hair like this!'

'All right. Please yourself. But before you do anything else clear the kitchen. It's getting impossible to move out here.'

At least the attic was ready; Polly had done that the day before. She took a few minutes off to check it while drying her hair. There was a gramophone, the table for serving drinks, the chairs. The bed under its striped blanket didn't look too bed-like. Her books were on the shelves, and her father had been persuaded to contrive a frame for Garth's mural fixing it to the wall.

She had a sudden thought and rushed downstairs, wet hair flapping.

'Sticks! I forgot sticks for the sausages! Do you think they'd sell them at the corner?'

'I doubt it,' sighed her mother. 'You'll just have to do without; you haven't time to go into the centre now.'

Amazingly, Mr. Devenish offered. 'I feel like some air,' he said, listening with an impassive face to his wife's list of possible shops. 'What are they drinking at this party?' he asked when she had finished.

'Polly's supposed to be making something.'

'Oh bordigals, I'd better do that next – but then what about the flans? And I've got to iron my dress some time.'

Her father departed.

'If the worst comes to the worst I'll do the flans,' said her mother. 'Calm down now, or you'll have a headache before it even starts.' She didn't mention that she had one herself.

'Thank you,' said Polly meekly.

'You could iron your dress next, then you'll be off the table when we need it for supper.'

Polly's dress was one she had made in the summer, straight sleeveless marigold cotton.

'Won't you be rather cold?' asked her mother.

'Not if I borrow that gorgeous white nylon shawl Aunt Sylvia sent Jonathan. It's hardly been used. I tried it on; it looks all right.'

'I'd have thought it would have been simpler to choose something with sleeves.'

'Everybody's seen all my things with sleeves.'

'Will you wear the shawl like a shawl or like a stole?' asked Jennifer.

'Like a shawl.'

'This is how you wear a stole.' Jennifer demonstrated with a teacloth. 'Sarah's sister's got one made of black mohair.'

'She must look like a mo.'

Hugh laughed himself on to the floor. 'A mo,' he said, rolling about under the table.

'Mind the flex,' said Polly.

Mark and Judith were the first guests to arrive, bringing the promised mugs in a basket.

'Is everything ready?' asked Judith.

'Sort of,' said Polly, looking a trifle wild. 'I'll just put these in the kitchen and then I'll take you up.'

'Can't I do anything to help?'

'It's too late now, we must go and be the party. Mummy's letting us leave the coats in their room, because I said the girls would need a decent mirror.'

'I thought Jonathan slept in there.'

'Not tonight.' Polly explained. 'He's supposed to be coming back if he's awful, but I don't think we need worry too much about that. I wouldn't put it past Mrs. Peabody to wake him just for the fun of giving him a cuddle.'

Penelope was the next to arrive. She was wearing pink with a full skirt, and her hair was tied back with a pink ribbon; Polly had never seen it out of plaits before. Her legs were clad in thin nylon and even her glasses had a festive look, since their frames happened to be pink too.

'I thought it was your birthday,' she said, slightly

breathless, 'but then Judith explained, so I brought a present for your room instead.'

Polly unwrapped a heavy glass mushroom.

'It's lovely. Chunky. Thanks awfully; you shouldn't have bothered, though.'

'I think it's a paperweight.'

Dad was the next to come, unrecognizable in a dark suit. Polly had just time to give him a drink and introduce him to the others before hearing Liz's penetrating voice in the hall. Hitching at her shawl she ran back downstairs.

'Coats in here. Liz, you've changed your hair!'

It hung raggedly to her shoulders and was a pale dull colour quite unlike its recent heather honey. Mouldy hay, thought Polly, pleased to see the living embodiment of Noyes' phrase.

'I've had it stripped,' said Liz, removing her coat. 'This is the new me. I'm going in for simplicity.'

Her dress was made of hessian, tied round the waist with a length of chain. She had bare feet and sandals, and no makeup at all.

'You sure are,' said Polly.

Upstairs Batty was talking to the Wilsons while Dad stood in a corner doubtfully eyeing the slice of cucumber that floated in his glass. He didn't seem to have drunk any yet. Liz joined him.

Several people arrived in quick succession and the room began to feel quite full. Polly worked hard ladling drinks, hindered by her shawl, which tended to dip its fringe into the large bowl.

Garth's mural was much admired.

'The colours fit the room so well,' said Liz.

'They could hardly help that, seeing it's painted from left-overs,' said Mark.

'Really?' Liz asked Garth. 'What a brilliant idea!'

Liz was larger than life tonight. Not that she wasn't always, but her new simplicity had done nothing to extinguish her. Polly was glad; everyone else seemed rather subdued.

'Tom did say he was coming, didn't he?' asked Judith.

'He did,' said Polly. Kim wasn't there yet either.

The conversation kept falling into holes. It was in one when Tom arrived; they all turned hopefully towards the diversion.

'H-hallo,' he stammered, made nervous by the expectant faces.

'Hallo; we were just wondering where you'd got to,' said Polly. 'Come and have some of my special recipe.'

'Is it fruit salad?' he asked, looking at the bowl.

This was too much for Sandy, whose splutterings infected everyone. At least it was better than silence, and Polly gave the scarlet Tom a quick smile.

'It's jolly good actually,' Sandy assured him. 'Won't poison you. It just needs putting through a sieve.'

'No, it's meant to have bits in,' said Boris.

'You know everyone,' Polly told Tom.

'Yes.' He glanced round and located Judith.

He was wearing her tie. When he had chosen it, in a fit of bravado, he hadn't anticipated her coming in the matching dress. Everyone would know they must be a pair and wonder why he didn't go near her. Keeping his hands down with an effort he turned to Sandy and Boris and continued the discussion of the fruit cup.

The last to arrive were Kim and Louise.

'I hope we're not late,' said Kim. Polly assured him they weren't.

'You look sweet in that shawl,' said Louise. She was breath-taking herself in a long slim trouser suit, made of dark blue velvet with a wonderful dusty bloom.

'I don't need it any more actually.' Polly shrugged it off before getting their drinks. 'The room's quite warm.'

'That's because of us,' said Tom. 'Every ten persons in a room is equivalent to one kilowatt.'

Sandy said: 'You mean you can have a fire without rubbing two boy scouts together?'

Polly hoped now everyone was there the party would really begin. She remembered the gramophone and put on one of the records borrowed from Liz, but nobody seemed to want to dance. She refilled all empty glasses and offered cheese straws round. Although there was quite a lot of noise from the two or three conversations going on together she had the impression that most people were listening to the one behind them in case it should be more interesting than theirs. Suppose they had supper an hour earlier than planned . . . it would still be ages before people could start to go home.

'You were at school with Polly, weren't you?' Kim asked Judith.

'Yes.'

'And with me,' said Louise.

'We're still there. Both of us,' said Batty. 'But it isn't the same without Polly.'

'I can imagine her absence might be felt.'

'Even the teachers that didn't like her are a bit lost with nobody to nag.'

'There are no other candidates?' Although he looked at Judith it was Batty who answered.

'Nobody quite the same.'

'I'm sure you all do your best.'

'Cheese straws?' asked Polly.

'Gosh, thanks. They look super,' said Batty. 'Did you make them yourself?'

'Yes.'

Judith took one but forgot to eat it; Louise, with a faint smile, refused.

'Delicious,' pronounced Kim. 'We were just discussing the gap you left in the dear old school. Apparently your friends are more law-abiding without you.'

'Is that what they said?' Polly asked, indignant.

'I don't think so,' said Judith abstractedly.

Turning away, Louise detached Dad from the neighbouring group. 'Do you like this music, Robert?' she asked. She never used his nickname.

'Like it? Oh. Yes. D'you?'

'I really prefer something like Joan Baez. Do you know Joan Baez?'

'No.' Dad looked round as though expecting to see her somewhere in the room.

'She's a Mexican-Irish singer.'

'Didn't think you could be both.'

'Judith didn't commit herself,' said Kim to Polly.

Judith appeared not to hear.

'O level chemistry's an easy exam,' Tom was saying.

'Really?' Sandy was missing none of the exchange between Louise and Dad, but unlike Judith he was able to listen and talk at the same time. 'Suppose they ask us the difference between air burning in coal gas and coal gas burning in air?' He prodded Boris. 'Bet you don't know.'

'I'm not expecting to get that question,' said Boris impassively.

'You should expect to get every question. Be prepared – isn't that the Boy Scouts' motto?'

'Yes,' said Tom. 'And the Girl Guides' motto is be prepared for Boy Scouts.'

'Cheese straws?' asked Polly.

They helped themselves liberally and she passed on, putting the plate down where it could be reached by Garth, Mark and Liz.

'Aha!' said Liz. 'Now we can settle the argument.'

'What argument?'

'Garth says you're a rebel. Mark says you're not.'

The two boys looked embarrassed. Polly thought on the whole she would prefer to be a rebel. On the other hand Mark had probably meant to compliment her; she wasn't so sure about Garth.

'I might have been once,' she compromised.

'Exactly what I said!' Mark was triumphant.

'What about *Lollipop Boy*?' asked Garth, flushing.

'Oh goodness, that wasn't much of a rebellion.'

'Now the day she dynamites the tech . . .' said

Liz. She munched a cheese straw and continued in a different tone: '"*Er – Miss Devenish – I think you've dropped the college*".'

'I wouldn't harm the tech,' said Polly. 'My old school perhaps.'

'And mine,' said Liz. She reached for another cheese straw, moving up and down on her heels in time to the music.

'We could dance if you like,' suggested Polly diffidently.

'We could dance!' agreed Liz with a pointed look at Mark and Garth.

The two boys eyed each other uneasily. The only partner either would consider worth the trouble was Polly; but in common politeness Liz must be asked first. Before Polly could speak she realized the whole room was silent. They had all heard Liz's challenge and nobody wanted to reply.

Polly minded more than Liz. It was her party. She considered all kinds of diversions before being provided with one of a most unexpected nature.

The five motor-cyclists had had some difficulty finding their way. They got the road all right; they were all agreed as to the road. It was over the house number that the uncertainties arose.

'Something in the seventies, did he say?'

'It had a nine in it, I know that.'

'Someone shoulda written it down.'

'Ner, we didn't know we'd be coming *then*.'

'It was twenty-seven,' said the smallest, but he went unheard.

'Just have to ride up and down until we spot it.'

'Yes. Ought to see something.'

'If we pushed the bikes we could listen,' said the smallest. The others roared away without replying, performed a spectacular turn at the end of the road and came roaring back to where the smallest stood by the gate of number 27.

'I can't hear anything,' he said.

'He's gone deaf. Isn't that a shame.'

The next gate opened and a boy came out wheeling a motor-cycle.

'Hey, we're looking for the party.'

'Polly's party?' said the boy, who was Ken Peabody.

'That's right.' Somebody trod warningly on the smallest's foot.

'In there,' said Ken. 'You from the tech?'

'Yes.'

They parked the five bikes in a row along the kerb, watched with interest by Ken.

'Quite a party she's having,' he said to himself as he rode away.

They rang the bell. What must be a younger sister opened the door.

'Hallo!' she said.

'We right for Polly's party?'

'Oh! Yes. It's at the very top of the house. I'll take you up.'

'What is this, Blackpool tower?' muttered one.

'That room's for coats,' she said on the landing, looking uncertainly at their leather jackets. 'The party's up there.'

'We'll keep 'em for now. Thanks.'

The quietness made them wonder if she could be kidding, but anyway they had to see. They tramped up the stairs one behind the other and entered a room full of frozen faces.

'Er – which one's Polly?' asked the leader.

'I am.' She watched in disbelief as more boys came through the door, until finally the fifth and smallest closed it behind them.

'You the wart charmer?'

'Ye-yes.' Oh no.

'Heard you were having this party,' said the leader in a rapid monotone. 'Thought we'd look in. Seeing how it was our money paid for it.'

'There's Alsop. Hi Robert!' said one of the other boys.

'Oh blimey,' said Dad.

'Five more boys,' announced Jennifer, returning breathless to the kitchen.

'Five?' said her mother, putting a hand to her back as she straightened up from the oven.

'Did they come on those motor-bikes?' asked her father.

'I thought everyone was here by now. Did you recognize any of them?'

'No.'

'I don't think we've got enough food for five extra.'

'Five great motor-bikes outside,' reported Mr. Devenish, returning from the front window.

'John, I suppose it's all right?'

'What did they look like?' asked Mr. Devenish.

'Rather rough,' said Jennifer.

'They wouldn't be gate-crashers, John?'

'I'll go up,' said Mr. Devenish with a sigh.

When he reached Polly's room he had some difficulty squeezing through the door, though as soon as they saw who he was they made a little space for him in the middle of the floor. There were certainly plenty of boys: all strangers to him apart from the three who'd helped with decorating that Saturday not long ago. He looked round the silent faces and said to Polly:

'Just thought I'd come and see if you needed . . . er . . . help with the drinks or anything like that.'

'Oh I'm managing, thanks.' Sparked into activity Polly lined up five glasses which had been replaced on the table, and filled them quickly before any of the newcomers could notice they weren't clean. She put in enough fruit to take up most of the space; she didn't see why she should waste her drink on them.

'That looks . . . um . . . interesting,' said her father. 'I'd quite like to try some myself.'

Polly gave him her own glass. She was wondering how on earth to get rid of the intruders, but it was hard to think with so many distractions. Dad, for instance, slumping so that his neck had vanished inside his jacket and looking as if he wished his head could follow – plainly he had talked too much at tech, and knew it. But the glare Mark was directing at Garth had no obvious reason.

Nobody spoke. The intruders tried to drink, hampered by the solid matter piling up against their lips. So long as Mr. Devenish stayed they were perfectly safe; neither they nor Polly wished to air the rights and wrongs of their case in front of him.

He sipped, and looked round the room again, feeling uneasily responsible for the silence. 'Let's see,' he said, 'I suppose one of you boys is Grandad.'

'Dad,' corrected Polly, pointing him out, whereat he looked unhappier than ever.

'I'm sorry. I knew it was a name betokening unlikely age.'

After a moment Tom said: 'Did you hear about the three old chaps being interviewed on the radio? They asked them all to what did they attribute their long life; and the first said' (Tom's voice took on a quaver) ' "I've never touched a cigarette since the day I was born." And how old are you, they asked? "Ninety-nine." The second said "I've never let a drop of alcohol past my lips." "And how old are you?" "A hundred and ten." The third said' (Tom's voice quavered so much it was barely audible) ' "I've always smoked fifty cigarettes a day, and drunk a bottle of whisky every night." "Good heavens. And how old are you?" "T-t-wenty-six!" '

There was a burst of laughter. Tom, pink with gratification, searched his memory for another joke; but for the first time in his life couldn't think of a single one.

The record came to an end and Polly changed it for something that looked loud. Her father winced as the violent rhythm ricocheted round the walls, and the leading intruder demanded a dance from Liz. She acquiesced without a word. Nobody else followed their example; instead they stood back to give them space. Coldly proficient, she danced through one piece and straight on into the next. And the next, and the next, and the next; her movements accurate and tireless, her skirt dipping and swinging in an exact rhythm, her eyes never leaving her partner's as he struggled with increasingly laboured breath to match her energy.

The LP side came to an end. 'What a pity,' said Liz, while Sandy clapped his applause.

'Well . . .' said Mr. Devenish to Polly, 'everything's all right then?'

'Fine.'

'Well, I mustn't stay any longer.' He went.

'You can go as well,' said Polly to the leather jackets. She looked for support to her friends, not all of whom were paying attention.

'I told you she was a rebel,' said Garth.

'You stupid damn fool!' replied Mark.

'Just a minute,' said Kim, stepping forward and waving one hand in a circular gesture for silence. 'Let's see if we can't sort this out quietly. The five of you think your money paid for the party, is that right?'

The leader gave a surly assent.

'So the first question is the amount of money involved. Polly?'

'I don't know which is which,' said Polly, looking at them and trying to remember the names on the postal orders. 'But that bunch added up to thirty shillings. There were six. One can't be here.'

'Dave wouldn't come because his were all gone,' said the smallest.

'Which brings us to the second question,' said

Kim. 'Has satisfaction been given? How much,' he asked the leader, 'did you pay?'

'Five bob.'

'That's how many warts?'

'They were sixpence each,' said Polly.

'Ten. Right then, show us your ten warts.'

'Well . . . I can't,' said the leader, indignation slowly dawning. 'Some have gone since then. Just shows what a fiddle it was – I paid to have 'em charmed and then they went by themselves.'

'Excuse me, you paid to have them charmed and they were charmed. Successfully.'

'But she didn't do anything!'

'She said so,' put in another. 'Robert told us.'

'And you believed it? With your warts gone? It didn't occur to you that she might be keeping her secrets?'

'All right then,' said the leader to Polly. 'What did you do?'

She hesitated, unsure why Kim's argument had taken its latest turn. He cut in coldly.

'You can hardly expect to be told now.'

'Anyway,' growled the other, defeated, 'like I said, they didn't all go.'

'Then, as I said, let's count them.'

He spread his hands and found four warts. 'There were six,' he kept saying, 'I know there were.'

'There were ten once,' replied Kim, unmoved. 'Let's see, that's two shillings you can claim.' He produced some change from his pocket. 'Here you are. Next?'

The others were quickly dealt with. The smallest

wouldn't take any money for his two remaining warts. 'They won't go if I do, will they,' he said, casting an awed glance in the direction of Polly.

At that one or two of his companions seemed about to start questioning the wisdom of their own behaviour, but Kim urged them out before an argument could develop. Polly crowded with the others to the window to watch the five motor-bikes roar away.

'Kim, I'll pay you back as soon as I've got it.'

'Don't worry. Cheap at the price.'

'And as for you,' said Mark to Garth.

'Mark,' said Judith.

He glared at her. 'Damn it, I'm not going to shut up! If I'd had any idea he'd involve Polly in a thing like that I'd have found some way to stop him when we first discussed it!'

Polly remembered the conversation they had had at Judith's house.

'As a matter of fact,' said Garth, 'I've done nothing. But if I'd wanted to you couldn't have stopped me. Who do you think you are?'

Mark changed tack. 'You're not going to pretend you didn't put the idea into Polly's head with your idiotic talk?'

'If I did it wasn't on purpose. I don't consider I own her the way you seem to. And you were the idiotic one. I suppose you still think charging people for successfully removing their warts is being dishonest in some mysterious sense?'

'There's nothing mysterious about it!' exploded Mark. 'She was damn lucky not to get into far worse trouble than she did!'

'I wish you'd stop talking about me as though I wasn't here,' said Polly.

'Do tell us now,' put in Judith quickly, 'did you actually do anything to charm the warts? Or not?'

'Not.'

'You gave them a belief for their money,' said Kim, 'but one couldn't really expect them to understand that.'

'I should think not,' muttered Mark, and: 'Apparently not,' sighed Garth.

'You made Polly sound quite a witch,' remarked Louise.

'She hasn't got the right colouring,' said Kim. 'Too fair.' He looked so thoughtfully at Louise's black hair and green eyes that he might just as well have made the comparison aloud. Polly almost felt sorry for her; she didn't seem to be having much of an evening as far as Kim was concerned.

'I'm thirsty,' said Liz. 'Where's my glass got to?'

'We'll have to wash some.'

Tom and Judith offered in the same breath and then both tried to withdraw, but Polly was already sharing the glasses between them. It was bad enough having Mark and Garth glowering in this ridiculous way; Tom and Judith could jolly well settle their differences while out of the room.

Dad, who had been trying to speak for some time, mumbled something in a low voice.

'He's sorry!' announced Sandy.

'Didn't think,' said Dad. 'When I mentioned your party, I mean. Never thought they'd *come*.'

'It doesn't matter,' Polly assured him handsomely.

Tom and Judith returned with the clean glasses and a happy air about them. Polly gave everyone another drink and felt things were beginning to go well.

'Let's play murder,' said Liz.

11

'Murder!'

'Oh *yes.*'

'That's a terrific idea.'

They began discussing different ways of drawing lots.

'Matchsticks, and you mark two.'

'Playing cards are better. Ace of spades is murderer.'

'I've got some playing cards,' said Dad, delighted to be of use. 'Always carry them about with me.'

'It is all right?' Liz asked, more brilliantly alive than ever. 'We can?'

'If you want to.' Polly was ruffled by their enthusiasm; she had been so sure nobody would care for party games.

She hadn't played murder for years, but when the cards were dealt she felt the authentic thrill of suspense. She was nothing; Tom was detective.

'We'll use all the first floor,' she said. 'Detective waits up here.'

She stood by the landing light as the players came filing down. 'When this goes off we start.'

The darkness was particularly black at first. There was no giggling; apart from occasional bumps and muffled gasps there were no sounds at all for the first few minutes. Then a child's voice, plaintive and disembodied, asked what was going on.

'Hugh! Why are you upstairs?'

'I'm in bed,' he said indignantly. 'And there are people prodding my toes.'

'Oh bother – it's all right, they're only playing murder. You don't mind, do you? If we keep out of your room? Okay everybody, this one's out of bounds.'

That seemed to settle Hugh; only as the game went on Polly occasionally sensed that someone unusually small was flitting about; breathing came from the wrong height, or there would be a patter of feet and the slam of a door just before the detective put on the lights. At least if it was Hugh he refrained from doing any murdering and managed not to get murdered himself.

The first time Sandy was detective he didn't get a chance to detect at all. Polly heard the gasp in Jennifer's room, but no cry of murder followed; instead the voice of Garth said 'You would, would you?' and there was a grunt, and Mark startled and furious asking 'What on earth?' and several more grunts and bangs, until the light was switched on and Kim stood there saying mildly:

'Now now, Polly's parents aren't going to like it if you fight over their heads.'

The two faced each other, breathing hard.

'What d'you expect if the corpse hits back?' said Mark.

'Serves you right,' muttered Garth, massaging the small of his back. 'I shouldn't be surprised if you'd injured my spine.'

'With that tap! Don't be ridiculous.'

'If that was a tap, so was what I gave you.'

'Good God, you don't imagine you hurt me, do you?'

Just then the voice of Mr. Devenish called from the hall.

'Polly, what's going on?'

'Nothing!' She glanced quickly at Kim, who stepped between the angry pair.

'Hmm . . . Have the motor-cycle contingent all departed?'

'Yes.'

He went away, and Sandy emerged from the attic. He was so indignant when he heard what had happened that they agreed he should be detective again and drew for another murderer, putting the lights off quickly lest Garth and Mark should resume their quarrel. This time he managed to get well into his investigation before being interrupted by Michael and Jennifer.

'What do you want?' said Polly.

'Bed.'

'Oh, not yet! Can't you wait a bit? We're in the middle of murder.'

They went back downstairs.

'I thought you were going to bed?' said their father.

'We can't,' said Jennifer. 'They're playing murder.'

'So that's what all the noise was,' said their mother. 'Well, they'll have to stop. You're late enough as it is.' Jennifer had been delighted to postpone her bedtime by putting sticks in sausages, making little extras from pastry trimmings, lining up mugs for soup, and taking the sticks out of the sausages again because they couldn't be cooked like that. 'Tell them to finish this one and then come down for their meal.'

When Michael and Jennifer arrived with their message Sandy had unmasked the murderer and cards had been drawn for the next round. 'All right,' said Polly. 'We'll be about a quarter of an hour.'

'They'd started another,' reported Jennifer.

'Then they can stop it.' Mr. Devenish moved towards the door.

'No don't, John. It's a shame to spoil things if they're going well. They are coming then, are they?'

'Oh yes,' said Jennifer.

'This is the last party she gives,' said Mr. Devenish. 'At any rate sit down while you're waiting.'

'I don't think I will.' Mrs. Devenish leaned thoughtfully against the cooker, where a large pan of soup stood ready. 'If I do I'll never get up again.'

Polly sidled into her old room and stood where the head of her bed had once been. She felt much safer if her back wasn't exposed. The curtained window was a square of dark grey in the blackness, and as she watched a tall black shadow crossed it. Involuntarily she shrank back. Somebody was breathing just beside her; somebody put out two hands, cupped her face, kissed her and was gone.

'M-murder?' said Polly doubtfully. Perhaps this had been going on all the time; perhaps Liz had only suggested the game to provide an opportunity. But nobody contradicted. 'Murder!' she called with more assurance.

The lights went on. Mark was detective.

'First I shall examine the body,' he said.

'Tut tut!' said Sandy.

'Nobody else did,' said Garth.

'There's no rule against it. A real detective could. Where was the wound?'

'On my – on my face,' said Polly. Sandy was delighted, though Mark seemed a bit taken aback.

'Bodies can't talk!' said Garth.

Mark rallied quickly. 'A real wound would show.'

Polly hoped to goodness hers didn't. She felt exposed enough already, and followed Mark's investigation with unusual interest. Eventually he narrowed it down to Garth or Kim. One of them was certainly lying. Under fierce cross-examination Garth grew more and more heated, but he stuck to his story. Kim answered gaily, casually; Polly was sure Garth had done it and wished Mark would stop trying to force a confession and simply accuse him. Eventually he did.

'No!' said Garth, triumphant.

'Me,' admitted Kim with a smile.

Mark didn't seem to mind being wrong. There was a general air of goodwill at the prospect of food; only Louise said: 'Well, that's that. These games do pall after a while, don't they.'

'I enjoyed all of it,' said Kim.

Polly shivered a little, from excitement she thought.

'Do you want your shawl?' Kim asked her.

'I don't think so.'

'But do wear it if I fetch it for you? You looked so nice shining through, like a Christmas lantern covered in snow.'

'Help, did I? All right. Thank you.'

Murmuring something about her hair she went into her parents' room and gazed at herself in the mirror. Her mouth looked very red; because, as she quickly realized, her face was rather pale.

Judith joined her.

'Have you and Tom decided to see each other again?'

'Yes,' said Judith.

'Good for you. I'm glad.'

'Doing without was much worse than I expected. It's funny, I can see in a way what my mother doesn't like about Tom – I mean apart from the things she's invented. But it doesn't make any difference to me. He's himself, and that's all about it.'

'Like Liz with Mr. Norris. She knows he's a twerp, but it doesn't matter.'

Like me with Kim, she thought. For a moment she wished she didn't care about Kim. Then the future couldn't hold a party where he behaved to her as he had to Louise this evening. She asked: 'How will you manage with your mother?'

'As best we can, I suppose.'

'That's the human condition,' said Polly with a giggle that astonished her by threatening to break into tears. She decided she had drunk too much fruit cup and changed the subject quickly. 'Whatever do you think's got into Mark and Garth? If they fight in front of my parents downstairs my father might think it was the last straw. Couldn't you say something to Mark?'

'Well no, I don't think I could. Don't you realize that what's got into them is you?'

'Me?' Polly was appalled.

'They're jealous of each other.'

'Oh no. Oh, how silly. What shall I do?'

'I don't see much you can do at the moment.'

'But if they wreck the party?'

'Let's hope it won't get that drastic.'

'You don't know my father when he loses his temper,' said Polly gloomily. 'Bordigals. Oh well. We'd better go down.'

Kim was waiting with her shawl and draped it round her shoulders. 'Just right,' he pronounced.

'I like that dress,' said Tom as Judith rejoined him.

'I likc that tic.'

Out of the kitchen came an intoxicating smell of hot soup and sausages. Michael and Jennifer passed by with wistful faces on their way to bed.

At the back of the table where the food was laid stood bottles of cider. 'Where did they come from?' asked Polly in astonishment.

'I got them when I went out for your sticks,' said her father shortly. He sounded as though he might since have regretted the impulse: both impulses.

'How lovely,' said Polly, grateful and meek. Taking a tray she went upstairs for the glasses and washed them quickly under the kitchen tap.

'I don't suppose this is all Polly's handiwork,' Kim was saying when she returned.

'I only did the trifle,' she admitted.

'I'm looking forward to the trifle. But everything is delicious,' he told Mrs. Devenish, taking a bite of flan. 'I can see where Polly learned her skill with cheese straws.'

'They turned out well, did they? They certainly looked pretty.'

'So does all this. You must have been awfully busy.'

Sandy was talking about advertisements. 'Buy Scrapeya! he declaimed. 'We may not be able to turn dirty old men into clean young men, but we can turn dirty young men into clean old men!'

Mr. Devenish, on his way out, laughed abruptly and said: 'You wouldn't remember the dirty old man on the Pears one. *A year ago I used your soap. Since then I have used no other.*'

Tom repeated this silently, filing it away for future use. Polly found herself next to Boris and asked on the spur of the moment: 'Is your mother really a Russian dancer?'

'No.' After a pause he said: 'She's Russian, though.'

'Can you speak it?'

'Not much.'

Liz was talking to Dad; she seemed to have taken him under her wing. Polly wondered why her mother looked so sleepy, then glanced at her watch and didn't wonder any more.

'I hope you don't mind us having the meal later than I said.'

'If you'd wanted it very much earlier it wouldn't have been ready. I suppose most people will be thinking of going soon?'

'Oh – well,' said Polly uneasily. 'Batty might have to, I suppose.' Penelope was losing her ribbon and looked hardly older than Jennifer; but not sleepy at all, rather the reverse. Polly edged away from her mother. She feared she might be working up to an announcement that everyone must go when supper was over. She wished her father would vanish but he was still in the room, consuming large quantities of food while talking to some of the boys.

Then Garth spilt a glass of cider down Mark's legs. Mark leaped backwards.

'You clumsy fool!'

Garth, about to apologize, set his lips in a line of defiance.

This is the end, thought Polly with dreadful calm.

'Yes, I'm so sorry, it was clumsy; I jogged his elbow.' Kim had pulled out a handkerchief and was stooping to wipe Mark's trousers. 'I think it'll be all right if it's sponged. I hope it wasn't the last of the cider; if it was, Garth must have mine.'

Over his head Mark and Garth eyed each other with identical feelings of resentment. Kim had been somewhat officious all evening. Polly didn't seem to mind at all; she was looking at him now with gratitude, even admiration – yes, definitely admiration, and a good deal more besides. Their eyes met again.

For the second time in as many minutes they shared the same thought and knew it.

'Don't worry,' said Mark automatically.

'It doesn't matter,' echoed Garth.

Polly fetched a cloth. Her father had gone; the food had mostly gone too. Kim began piling used plates together.

'It was very good,' he said again to Mrs. Devenish.

'Keep your glasses,' Polly advised them. 'There's a bit of fruit cup upstairs.'

'We'll remember the children are in bed,' said Kim. 'No more noisy games.'

It was all right; her mother wasn't objecting. Polly rushed the plates into the kitchen and started a move back to the attic before any more could be said.

Kim found a record and asked if he could put it on.

'Let's dance,' he said to Polly.

'Well . . . if the others . . .'

'They will if we do.'

For a moment she thought it would be like the time with the black corduroy boy when her legs had refused to move. Furious with herself she looked at Kim and pretended nobody else was there. It worked.

The others did join in: Tom with Judith, and Mark, very surprised at his own temerity, with Louise.

'Oh go on,' said Sandy to Boris, 'just a dance.'

'No. I'm asking her.'

Sandy watched in cheerful amazement as Boris

claimed Penelope. 'That leaves you and me,' he told Liz. 'I don't fancy either of the other two, do you?'

Garth and Dad looked morose at his wit.

Kim danced once with Louise. Tom, privately persuaded by Judith, danced once with Penelope. Liz gave Dad a lesson; Polly wondered if she found something appealing in his mournful pale-lipped face and curranty eyes.

'What does that intriguing little curtain conceal?' asked Kim, sitting on the bed to rest.

'It's my sky window,' said Polly. 'For watching the stars when I'm in bed.' She pulled one cord.

'No stars,' said Kim, lying back across the striped blanket, 'but look, there's the moon.'

Polly lay back as well. 'How clever of it to be just there!'

'The moon, or the window?'

'The moon, I meant. I suppose I could have meant the window.'

'I like these plushy tassels.'

'They're dressing-gown cords.'

'Used you to think dressing-gown only had one g?'

'Oh, it should,' said Polly at once. 'Like bustop. And bustation.'

'Bustation is a splendid word.'

'It might be a course at the tech: corsetry and bustation.'

She noticed Louise looking at them as they laughed, and pulled herself back to a sitting position. Kim did the same. He ended up closer than before.

'You were tremendous with those motor-cycle boys,' she said.

'Necessity. I don't think they would have improved the party, do you?'

'*No.*'

'You've got nice parents. Easy-going.'

'It was touch and go they didn't turn everyone out after supper. That was thanks to you, too.

'It's a very good party.' Kim found her hand and squeezed it to emphasize his words.

Polly hoped the others thought so as well. At that moment Louise was the only one unoccupied. Penelope and the boys were having fun with a wooden jigsaw Sandy had found in the bathroom, timing each other to see who could do it fastest.

Kim made a long arm and picked up her glass mushroom.

'Batty brought it. A present for my room.'

'Nice idea. Batty's the infant in specs?'

'She's older than she looks – a bit older,' murmured Polly. 'She rather took to you, I think.'

Kim appeared to consider this no more than his due. 'Judith seems happy,' he said idly.

'So does Tom.'

Feet sounded on the stairs and Polly's father opened the door.

'A Mr. . . . Mannering? The father of Louise . . . has just telephoned,' he said, glancing round the faces until Louise caught his eye. 'He says he'll be here to collect you in about fifteen minutes.' He withdrew.

'Why on earth is he doing that, I wonder!' said

Louise, thoroughly put out. 'Kim would have taken me home.'

Kim said nothing. Polly tried to disengage her hand, but was not allowed.

'Or I could have gone with Robert.'

Dad blushed from his place next to Liz on the window seat and mumbled that he wasn't going straight home.

'It's immaterial now in any case,' snapped Louise.

Penelope looked at the time and said in dismay that she should be leaving too. Louise grudgingly offered a lift.

They heard a car draw up outside and Polly escorted the two girls downstairs.

'The coats are in here,' said Mr. Devenish. 'Your mother's in bed, and I'm going as well now. Time everybody left.'

'All right,' said Polly.

Her mother would have seen them all out of the house; her father, having delivered the order, left them to get on with it. Polly was able to return to her guests, explain the position, and allow Kim's request for a last dance. He had found a waltz record at the bottom of the pile of pop. Apart from Tom and Judith nobody else danced, but Polly wouldn't have minded being the only couple now.

When they opened the attic door the house below was in darkness. Liz, considerately tiptoeing, lost a sandal between two treads of the stairs and scrabbled for it in the shadows of the landing until Polly thought to put the light back on.

Downstairs they buttoned their coats and paid low-voiced compliments about the party.

'I had a scarf,' said Kim vaguely.

'You'll need it, mate.' Sandy turned his collar up. 'Come on Boris, got your earmuffs? See you next term, all.'

'Some,' said Boris, following.

'I certainly thought I had a scarf,' said Kim, looking round the table where the coats had been piled.

Liz and Dad went off together, Mark with Judith and Tom.

'Good-bye,' said Garth heavily, wishing Polly would give him a little attention instead of searching for Kim's belongings. He didn't know why he had stayed so late; there would no doubt be an unpleasant exchange with his grandfather when he got in. 'Good-bye,' he repeated with even greater significance.

'Good night,' said Polly, and closed the door behind him. 'I wonder what on earth they've done with that scarf?'

'Well never mind,' said Kim, following as she wandered in and out of the rooms and exclaiming involuntarily at the state of the kitchen.

'It is rather, isn't it,' agreed Polly.

'Imagine tomorrow morning.'

'I shouldn't think I'll see much of the morning.' She yawned, suddenly feeling in all her bones the lateness of the hour.

'Then we'd better do it now,' he said briskly. 'You can't leave it all to someone else.'

She watched, incredulous, as he rolled up his sleeves and turned on the tap.

'Right?' he said.

'Right,' said Polly, banishing her sleepiness without difficulty in order to fall in with his mood. They talked while they worked, and it was satisfying to see the change they made in the kitchen.

'Surprise for your mother,' said Kim.

'I must say you're awfully considerate towards my mother.'

'Surprise for you?'

'Well I did think —'

'You did think . . . ?'

'I *did* wonder if you were particularly polite at supper because you wanted the party to go on.'

'I was. So this makes up.' He dried his hands while Polly considered his answer and decided she liked it.

' "Christmas is coming," ' he sang softly. 'Christmas is a pretty close season in my family, but I'm getting out to a party for New Year.'

Polly wondered why she had to be told. She felt like stopping her ears before he could say the party was to be given by Louise.

'Partners optional,' he said. 'Would you like to come?'

'Oh!'

'Think it over and let me know. Now where's my coat?'

'I've thought it over. I would like to come.'

'Good.' He patted his pocket and felt inside. 'And good again; here's my scarf.'

He tucked it neatly round his neck and then kissed her.

'The other one didn't count,' he said.

There was something she had been wanting to ask. 'Did you know it was me? In the dark?'

'Of course. I tracked you down by your scent.'

'How predatory.'

'Oh I am. Good night, Polly.'

'Good night.'

If you have enjoyed this book you may also like these:

RICH AND FAMOUS AND BAD *by Rodie Sudbury* 30p

552 52027 6

Polly and Judith scorned their classmates' interest in boys. They preferred Judith's brother and his friends to keep out of their way. Then Judith's feelings changed – and Polly invented the kind of boy she would like to know. But soon she finds her fantasy world turning into a frightening reality, and her daydream of being 'rich, famous and bad' turns into a nightmare.

TO VANISHING POINT *by Doreen Norman* 20p

552 52003 9 Carousel Fiction

There was a strange glow in the playground. Leaves were blowing round on the ground, but in a perfect circle. Then Hazel noticed something else, something which, somehow, no-one but herself could see. A girl was standing looking at her, a silver girl from another planet.

JASON *by Joyce Stranger* 20p

552 52004 7 Carousel Fiction

The pup wasn't wanted, born of a golden Labrador bitch and a giant mastiff. Then Duncan found him, a lonely young boy who needed a friend just as much as Jason needed a loving owner. The closeness between them was only strengthened when Duncan was sent away to school, and then his father had an accident, Jason had to do something.

HAVELOK THE WARRIOR *by Ian Serraillier* 20p

552 52007 1 Carousel Fiction

These are the days when evil men conspired to overthrow the monarchy, greedy for the power and wealth of wearing the crown and ruling the land. The King of Denmark is dead, his son Havelok forced to flee the murderous attempts of Earl Godard by escaping to the shores of England. He grows up to be a great warrior, to recover his kingdom.

THE STORY OF MAUDE REED *by Norah Lofts* 25p

552 52010 1 Carousel Fiction

Her grandfather was only a wool merchant and his house was not considered suitable for a young girl of noble blood. Maude was now old enough to be taught the accomplishments of a lady; sewing, music and the art of graceful behaviour. But this was the Fifteenth Century, and her school was to be an old, dark castle.

THE GYPSY'S GRAND-DAUGHTER 25p
by Margaret Dunnett

552 52023 3

Kate's grandmother was a gypsy, and her Romany ways attracted Kate. But her mother led a very conventional life. Gradually Kate found herself being drawn away from her normal home life towards her other self, the 'gypsy's grand-daughter'. It was then that a deep conflict arose, between her love for the gypsies and her mother's respectability. . . .

THEFT *by Wendy Robertson* 25p

552 52025 X

In a working class town in the North, three young children find some books and gold coins in a shed behind the local pub. They take them, but soon their conscience makes them return their find. And when they do so, they witness a real robbery, which poses a problem: 'We couldn't get help 'cos the the cops would be asking what we were doing out here in the middle of the night.'

THE GOD BENEATH THE SEA 30p
by Leon Garfield & Edward Blishen

552 52031 4 Carousel Fiction

This is one of the most important children's books since the war. Winner of the Carnegie Award for children's literature in 1970, and runner-up for the Kate Greenaway Medal, the book is a dramatic, forcefully poetic retelling of the classic Greek myths. It covers the creating of the Gods, the making of man, and the Gods' struggles to control man; into this vast canvas are woven a succession of myths such as the flood, Prometheus, Sysyphus and a multitude of others. This epoch-making book is supported by Charles Keeping's remarkable illustrations.

LOOKING AND FINDING *by Geoffrey Grigson* 25p

552 54007 2 Carousel Non-Fiction

You can find sunken treasure, hidden away in some long-forgotten shipwreck, or discover the past through scattered fossils and ancient inscriptions. It depends what you're looking for, how you go about finding it. It depends where you're looking, how you go about getting there. But once the search begins, there's no knowing what you might stumble across.

THE WHITE BADGER *by Gordon Burness* 25p

552 54008 0 Carousel Non-Fiction

A badger was born just outside London, in fact only eighteen miles from the city centre. He was discovered by eleven year old Gary and his older brother Phil, who had arrived one day at the author's doorstep with a request to be taken badger hunting. There first find was unusual, for it wasn't an ordinary badger, it was all-white, an albino badger. Gary called him Snowball, and this is his story.

NATURE DETECTION AND CONSERVATION 25p
by Jean Mellanby

552 54019 6

Nature and wild life are today threatened by a variety of man-made dangers such as industrial pollution. This serious problem has baffled our top scientists and politicians. Yet there is plenty that you can do about it, and this book shows how we can all become nature detectives and help preserve wild life, even if we live in the heart of a city. And we can enjoy doing so.

PARADE OF HORSES *by Vian Smith* 30p

552 54022 6

This is the book for all who love horses, In his affectionate journey through the world of horses, Vian Smith tells of farm-horses and steeplechasers, circus horses, and the breeds which have disappeared over the years such as the fire and funeral pairs. Included are eight pages of photographs, and numerous drawings of different horses.

These books are available at bookshops and newsagents. If you have difficulty finding them you can buy them by post from the following address:

TRANSWORLD PUBLISHERS LIMITED
P.O. Box 11, Falmouth, Cornwall.

Please send with your order a cheque or postal order (not currency) to cover the cost of the book, plus 6p for each book ordered to cover the cost of postage and packing.